Unexpected Grace

Unexpected Grace

A Life in Two Worlds

Farifteh V. Robb

First Edition: 2017

ISBN: 978-0-9965168-9-1

[LS-20170310-TS30]

Great Writing Publications
www.greatwriting.org
Taylors, SC, USA

Dedication

For my children and their children

Contents

Acknowledgements

I am greatly indebted to the following persons:

Simon Holt, who encouraged me to begin writing; Jim Holmes, editor and publishing consultant at www.greatwriting.org, for his patient guidance, valuable suggestions and professional expertise; and my husband James, without whose support this memoir could not have been written.

Author's Note

Insofar as this memoir touches on recent history and political developments in Iran, the author's sole intention has been to provide a personal perspective and reflection on these events as they were experienced by her at the time.

Preface

For a number of years my family have been asking me to recount the story of events which have shaped my life. It has taken me a quarter of a century to find the courage to do so. Until now my reluctance has been the fear of portraying events inaccurately, the fear of offending peoples' feelings, and the fear of censure. These fears still lurk somewhere within me, but I am now a different person and finally ready to acknowledge the reconciliation of my two worlds.

I was born *farangi*, in Geneva, Switzerland, in the winter of 1950. *Farangi* is a Persian word meaning 'European'. My name 'Farifteh' ('loved to distraction') is pure Persian, but I was also given a *farangi* middle name, 'Valentine', from the saint on whose commemorative name-day I was due to be born. This name was recorded in my Iranian birth certificate even though middle names are not customary in Iran. When my sister arrived two years later she too was given a European middle name. There was no doubt in my parents' minds that being born in *Farang* was an advantage not to be ignored.

Growing up *farangi* in a Persian family in Switzerland and attending an international school meant that my sister and I became trilingual—able to converse effortlessly in Persian (*Farsi*), French and English. On visits to Iran this skill, along with our European manners, was always much admired, and my parents would bask in the knowledge that we were truly blessed to have had a *farangi* start in life. However, despite this auspicious beginning, things didn't turn out as they had envisaged, and we sisters have ended up with very different lives. The Islamic Revolution of 1979 in Iran cut a great swathe through the social order, distanced many families, and changed ordinary lives for ever. Powerless to stem its tide, the events which followed the Revolution separated us and our paths circumstantially diverged. Sadly now, a gulf exists between us—I have become quintessentially European, while she, perhaps somewhat reluctantly, is completely Iranian. We have each lost what might have been.

This Memoir is the story of one such changed life—my own. I have written it for my children, and their children's children, that they might know something of their roots, and understand my life's journey. My own parents, like many of their generation, were economical in recounting their past lives, and much of their history is now regrettably lost. Until recently, I, too, have been similarly guarded in describing my experiences of conversion from Islam and my life in Iran during the Revolution in any detail. My hope is that this Memoir will go some way in redressing that situation. It is not an exhaustive autobiography, but primarily a reflection on the more memorable events in my life.

I continue to inhabit two worlds—the Persian and the *farangi*. At times I have attempted to ditch one in favour of the other, but both remain resolutely integral to my psyche, and ultimately they have intertwined to make me the person I have become. It is this reconciliation which bestows upon me the unexpected gift of an abundant grace.

Edinburgh, 2017

Baba and Mami, Birmingham, 1948

BABA AND MAMI

People often ask me, 'Whatever happened to the name "Persia"?' a name evocative of roses, nightingales, carpets and cats, while 'Iran' conjures up uneasy images of stern-faced mullahs and gun-wielding extremists. But Iran has always called itself by this name which means 'Land of the Aryans'. In the early twentieth century Reza Shah, father of the last Shah of Iran, led his country into a modernisation programme which involved sweeping changes to the social order, industrial reforms, and the casting aside of an agrarian way of life which had dominated the kingdom for generations. The old order was based on a hierarchy which had bequeathed stability to Persian social mores for centuries. Now, overnight it seemed, gone was the society where there was a universally accepted code of dress, behaviour, and etiquette. For now the *farangi* way of life was 'in', and West, it seemed, had become the new Best.

My parents, Baba and Mami, were unusual for middle class Iranians of their generation in that had they had met in Tehran but had married in England in the late 1940s. There was a difference of seventeen years between their ages, which meant that Baba was getting old when Mami was only entering middle age. Baba was born in 1905 and remembered the advent of World War I. He was raised in Semnan, a provincial town on the plains of north-eastern Iran at a time when Iran was still an agrarian country governed by feudal laws. Mami was born in Tehran in 1922. She was a city girl and a child of World War II.

My respective grandfathers were both physicians of the Persian old school. Baba's father was an eighth-generation doctor prominent in local affairs. His extensive knowledge of illnesses and traditional remedies meant that he was a well-respected member of Semnani society, and he was accorded the honorary accolade of *Hafez-e-Seheh* which means 'Protector of Health' in Arabic, then the lingua franca of learned Persians. His own father had been known by the honorary title of *Montakhab-al-Attebâ* ('Chosen Among Physicians'). Decades later when the Iranian government decreed that all citizens should adopt a Western-style surname excluding soubriquets such as *Haji* ('pilgrim of Mecca'), *Seyyed* ('descendant of the Prophet') or *Mirza* ('nobleman'), he chose *Hafezi* as his family's surname, the suffix "*i*" being a descriptive patronymic indicating descent from the *Hafez* line.

My grandfathers: left: paternal, right: maternal

Mami's father was a doctor in downtown Tehran. Always respectfully known as *Aghayé Doktor* ('Mister Doctor'), he practised a combination of homeopathy and public health, laced with a liberal dose of common sense. A small photograph of each grandfather exists, probably taken in the 1930s—both men were obviously important enough to warrant posing for this new portrait technology. My Semnani grandfather, elderly and benign, wears a crumpled Western-style linen jacket, shirt and tie; my Tehrani grandfather, balding with a natty moustache, is also dressed in a European suit and sports a handkerchief in his left breast pocket.

Baba grew up in a traditional household in Semnan, a dusty provincial town on the caravan route to the holy city of Mashhad. His home was built around a courtyard with its small central pool. In the outer courtyard were the men's quarters, known as *biruni* ('outside'). Here men sat, drank tea, chatted, ate, smoked their water-pipes, recited verse, and received visitors. Within the courtyard were the inner women's quarters known as *andarun* ('inside'), the domestic heart of the home, a set of interconnecting rooms protected on all sides by the patriarchal quarter. It included the kitchen, the chicken run, and an outhouse with its hole-in-the-ground toilet. The central room housed the all-important *korsi*, a traditional Persian indoor source of heat which is a low table under which a brazier is filled with hot coals and over which a thick blanket is draped. A tray containing the *samovar* (a tall metal urn to boil water) and teapot is placed on top. Around this family and visitors alike could sit and socialise.

Baba's mother had died when he was very young. He had an older sister and several step-siblings from his father's remarriage. Because of his mother's illness he had been wet-nursed by a local woman. In later years I met an elderly gentleman who was respectfully introduced to us as Baba's *hamshireh* or 'milk brother'. He was not a relation, but as the wet-nurse's own son he was considered to be honourably related, since suckling from the same breast was deemed to create a bond as strong as a blood tie. Provincial Iran in the first part of the twentieth century was still in the grip of nomadic tribes, and marauding horsemen sometimes rode into town to engage in skirmishes with one another. When this occurred womenfolk would rush out to gather their children to safety. Baba remembered several occasions when he was scooped up and bundled along with a number of other small children and hidden in the cavernous depths of the communal *tanoor* ('oven') which had cooled down after the day's bread had been baked.

The Iran of Baba's youth was nevertheless culturally secure and steeped in traditions which had remained unchanged for generations. People knew where they stood in the social hierarchy and everyone followed the strict codes of Persian etiquette without question. Persian etiquette is based on lofty ideals of politeness and hospitality, and infringement is often taken as a discourtesy. There is, for instance, the superiority of age. The greater your age, the higher is your status and the more deferential your treatment. Elders are at the top of this social pyramid, while children are at its opposite end. Children are taught from an early age not to sit at the top end of a room in a social gathering. This area is considered to be *bâla* ('high'); it's usually furthest from the door, with the nicest end of carpet and the most comfortable chairs. The doorway area or *pâ'een*, ('below') is likely to be draughty and usually reserved for children and younger family members. Two separate incidents from Baba's childhood illustrate how an ingrained observance of Persian etiquette could at times be taken to extremes, and how it could also hide an undercurrent of intolerance, sometimes unfairly so.

The first incident is about Baba's elder sister who had been recently married and was the new mother of an infant boy. Her in-laws lived several *farsangs* (a Persian measure of distance equivalent to about four miles) distant from Semnan. They had not yet met their first grandchild and had proposed a visit. For days my aunt had busied herself cleaning the house and cooking meals, but her baby fell ill with a high fever. Before the advent of antibiotics there was a local saying: *'bacheyé avval mâlé kalâghé'* ('the firstborn belongs to the crows') — crows being portents of doom. A poultice was applied, prayers were said, and the baby appeared to rally. As Baba's sister anxiously rocked the cradle on the appointed day, a cloud of dust was spied in the distance from the horses' hooves and the *droshkeh* (open carriage) on the desert road. Suddenly the baby stopped whimpering, turned ashen grey and lay completely still. In that instant my aunt knew that her infant son had died. But so deeply instilled was her sense of propriety and hospitality that, instead of running wailing from the door to break the terrible news, she swallowed her grief and pretended that her child was merely sleeping. A dutiful daughter-in-law, she stepped out to welcome her husband's parents in the manner befitting their status. Pleasantries were exchanged and tea dispensed. Her in-laws admired their sleeping grandchild from a distance dictated by the fever, and after a brief and formal visit said their farewells, satisfied that their son had made a good match—his bride knew how to run a well-appointed and hospitable home, and as a bonus had also quickly produced a son. My aunt watched until their *droshkeh* was again a speck of dust on the horizon. Only then did she fall on the ground giving vent to grief, beating her breast and wailing inconsolably. The remarkable fact is that such behaviour was almost expected and not considered to be out of the ordinary. Many of Baba's relatives, on being informed of what had happened, merely commented: 'Well, of course, that is exactly how a true *khânum* ('lady') would behave.'

The second incident relates to the castigation of a neighbouring family who through no real fault of their own had fallen upon hard times. One of their sons had unfortunately become a *tariâki*, ('drug addict'). To fund his habit he had sold everything his family possessed, piece by piece, leaving them destitute in a house devoid of all furniture. At last, desperate for more cash, he even dismantled the large ornate gate from his family's *biruni* and sold that too, thus shamefully exposing their new poverty-stricken existence to all passers-by in the street. The Semnani elders muttered and shook their heads over tea and backgammon, while reproaching the innocent neighbours behind their backs for having somehow fostered disrespect and poor manners within the family which had brought about this dishonour and fall from grace.

On the other hand, it is inherent consideration for the wellbeing of strangers which redeems true Persian hospitality from any perceived superficiality. Iran has an age-old Zoroastrian tradition relating to the 13th day of *Nowruz* (Persian New Year, celebrated on the first day of Spring) when it's unlucky to stay indoors. Known as *Sizdah bé-dar* ('Thirteen Out-of-doors') it is a day when whole families universally decamp to the countryside to enjoy a picnic. Baba remembered one particular *Sizdah bé-dar* when Semnan's local *kalântari* ('police station') had a single prisoner, a thief, in its cells. Rather than leave him indoors and prey to the Evil Eye which is traditionally believed to lurk indoors on the unlucky thirteenth day seeking to cause misfortune or injury, they walked their prisoner to the picnic site. While children played among the rocks and grown-ups spread rugs under the trees and brought out the food, the *kalântars* tied him loosely to a cypress tree. There he rested in the shade, being fed delicacies from everyone's dishes—a bonus day out. Consideration for the feelings of others is Persian etiquette at its very best.

When Baba was ten years old a *rammâl* or fortune teller prophesied that he would one day become a doctor. On a hot summer day he and two lads who were brothers were playing near the dry riverbed in Semnan when they encountered a youth who practised geomancy. For a few coins he tossed his dice, and from the lie of stones and lines in the dirt he foretold that each of them would achieve great things: my father would cure the sick, the elder of the boys would become close to the Sultan, and his brother a warrior. This prophecy did indeed come to pass: Baba went to medical school, the older boy became a senator in the Shah's new parliament, and his brother joined the army where he rose to the rank of general. The *rammâl* collected his coins and went on his way. What neither he nor any of the lads could have foreseen was that one day their worlds would come crashing round them, and that there would be neither Sultan nor Shah to lead the country, and not even a kingdom remaining.

There was only one educational establishment in Semnan, and it was for boys only. Baba attended the primary department known as the *maktab* where basic literacy and numeracy were drummed into pupils by an inordinate volume of copying and rote learning. Subjects taught depended on the skills and interests of their teacher. One of Baba's schoolmasters decided to teach the boys the basics of engineering. This subject was eagerly anticipated by the boys but lessons ended abruptly when it became clear that they were unable to attain the first requisite which involved the ability to draw a long and perfectly straight line in Indian ink without the help of a ruler. This skill had to be mastered first as the bridges and dams which they might be called upon to design in the brave new Iran could end up uneven or lopsided. Why were rulers not allowed? The reason given, Baba said, was that they might not always have all the necessary tools and instruments at their disposal in the desert, and they must be able to 'make do' without them! The boys therefore spent an entire term attempting to draw straight lines freehand. Baba was finally able to do this with his eyes closed and looked forward to the next lesson. But after the holidays that particular schoolmaster left town and the boys never progressed beyond this point in engineering studies.

From the *maktab* Baba graduated to the *dâr-al-f'noon*, which served as a secondary school, and after that he travelled to Tehran to study medicine. Upon qualifying as a doctor he first became an adviser at the new Ministry of Health, and subsequently accepted a scholarship from Reza Shah's government to go abroad to study Public Health, choosing England as his destination. Most of his contemporaries who gained one of these prestigious grants chose to go to France, since the old Persian legal and fiscal systems were based on French models and at that time French was the second language in Iran. But Baba had read and admired the popular book *Self Help* (1859), by the Scottish philanthropist and philosopher Samuel Smiles, and had been inspired by its portrayal of sterling British character-building values such as perseverance, civility, independence and individuality. It was for him a turning point.

Baba as a young doctor in London

Baba first went to London in the summer of 1936, arriving at the height of the abdication crisis of Edward VIII. It was a world away from the sun-baked fig orchard of his father's house and the shady walnut and pistachio trees that dotted the dusty streets of his native Semnan. His journey to England from Iran was by rail across Turkey and Russia—a journey that seemed to take forever. It was, in effect, a voyage that crossed not only the east-west cultural divide, but which also bridged an agrarian way of life and the new industrial age. From Tehran Baba made his way north to Russia where he boarded a Trans-Siberian train that rattled across the northern steppes of Russia and the arid valleys of Ottoman Turkey before stopping for a few hours in Constantinople. Baba was not unused to the sight of poverty, but even he was shocked at the ragged state of Russian peasantry where in the railway stations, barefoot women were employed to shovel snow and dirt from the tracks. Baba thought a country must really be desperate if it sent its womenfolk out barefoot in all weathers to sweep snow. In his dominantly patriarchal world women were considered to be weak and subservient, but if weak they were also to be cherished and protected. The seemingly interminable journey across Europe passed in a blur, but Baba retained a vivid recollection of finally arriving in Paris at the Gare Saint-Lazare at night. It was raining, and the street lights of Paris twinkled in the dark. Electricity was as yet to arrive in Semnan, and Baba was completely entranced by what seemed to be 'fairy lights' all around him. He could not stop looking down at these shiny dancing stars reflected in the wet pavements. From Paris Baba made his way to Dieppe and then across the English Channel to Newhaven.

Billeted with a landlady not far from the Mall, everything appeared strange to him—the small dark houses, the soot-laden chimneys, the cold and damp weather, and the thick swirling London fog. Memories of sunny poetry recitals among the cypress trees of Semnan now were a world away, but Baba was keen to better himself and he threw himself enthusiastically into the business of getting to know this new *farangi* world. Among his early recollections were watching the changing of the guard at the gates of Buckingham Palace and seeing a kilted regiment marching past. 'Who are they?' he mused out loud, not having seen men in skirts before. 'That's the Middlesex, mate!' a bystander incorrectly informed him. 'Ah,' he thought to himself wryly, 'in England, there are men, there are women, and there is also "middle sex"!'

Meanwhile he first had to become fluent in English, matriculate, and sit the entrance examinations for Medicine. Baba's entry into the training scheme was not as straightforward as it had seemed when his acceptance papers had come through in Iran. Already a qualified doctor, his traditional Persian medical qualification from Tehran University wasn't considered adequate in the English system, and he was obliged to complete the final three years of undergraduate medicine and surgery at University College Hospital in London prior to studying at 'The Tropical', as the London School of Hygiene and Tropical Medicine was locally known. The first hurdle was matriculation. For this he was required to pass the final school board examinations in literacy and numeracy. Baba duly applied. The problem was his mastery of English which was as yet fairly rudimentary. He managed to pass the literacy paper where he had to write an essay titled 'What I would do if I had five guineas'. He did rather well at this, considering that his reflections were based on the experiences of a thirty-year-old graduate, and not merely the saving of pennies for sweets or a bicycle. The maths paper was a different challenge. It contained a problem involving the speed of falling hailstones. Baba raised his hand to ask the meaning of the word 'hailstone'. 'No questions,' intoned the invigilator with a masklike expression on his face. Never one to accept defeat, Baba did his calculations but wrote in the margin of his paper: 'I don't know what a hailstone is, but I have done the sum by assuming that each hailstone weighs 15lb.' He passed.

A few years later, having finally requalified as a doctor in the British system, he returned to Iran to work at the Ministry of Health in Tehran. There he became acquainted with one of the young secretaries—Mami. But their friendship then was solely on a formal footing.

⁓✦⁓

Unlike Baba who was born almost a generation earlier, Mami's youth was spent in the eye of Reza Shah's cultural reforms. *Aghayé Doktor,* my Tehrani grandfather, was a strict disciplinarian who ruled his household with a rod of iron. His three sons (one died in infancy) and three daughters knew him as a kindly but remote autocrat whose word was law. They lived in a three-storeyed brick house at the end of an alley in downtown Tehran, and in keeping with his status as a physician, *Aghayé Doktor* ran his household along fairly progressive lines. Meals were taken at a dining table with knives and forks—then relatively unusual in Persian households where a family traditionally sat on the floor round a cloth spread on the carpet and ate using their fingers and spoons. A dining table was considered to be very *farangi*. Mealtimes often ended in tears, however, as even a minor misdemeanour signalled immediate expulsion to the kitchen to sit among the servants. Mami remembers numerous occasions when one after another she and her brothers and sisters were relegated outside until only her father and mother remained seated at either end of their grand table.

As the youngest in a large household Mami felt generally unnoticed. Particularly fond of her father she strove hard to become his favourite. One successful ploy was to lie in wait for the *yakhi* or street ice seller to arrive with his mule and cart shouting out loudly *'âyy yakh'*, announcing his wares. During the hot summer months, oblong blocks of ice were hewn from the *qanâts* (underground water stores) deep in the mountain foothills above Tehran where they had been left to freeze during the cold winter months. Frozen *qanât* water would be dug out and hawked round the city streets by *yakhis* who would stop at houses and help to carry the block into the kitchen area where it could be chipped with ice hammers and stored in earthenware pitchers. Prior to the advent of refrigeration, every house aspired to have a *yakhchâl* or ice pit to keep perishables fresh. As soon as Mami heard the *yakhi* calling she would run up the alley with sheets of newspaper to take delivery of their daily ice block. Once home she would wrap it carefully in layers of newspaper, further insulate it with a blanket, and then hide it in the coolest place she could think of—usually underneath their horsehair settee. All afternoon she would nurse her ice block, trying to keep it from melting by renewing the layers of newspaper and guarding it from anybody intent on chipping off bits of ice to suck. As soon as her father appeared she would knock off a large chunk with the ice hammer, deposit it in a tall glass with sherbet cordial and put a fresh mint leaf on top. This she would present to her father, who invariably patted her head and told her what a good child she was.

Although Mami lived in the city, she seems to have had more encounters with animals and wildlife than Baba who was raised in the country. Stray cats and dogs roamed in every city street. Dogs are considered as *najess* ('unclean') in Islam and were universally shunned, but stray cats were sometimes adopted as pets. Mami loved cats. One particular feline was taught by her to feed itself politely by dipping a paw into food and licking it clean. Such was the dexterity of this adopted puss that it was even allowed its own place at the family dining table. One hot afternoon during the siesta Mami watched her cat come face-to-face with a snake that had slithered out of a hole in the dry stone garden wall. Puss bravely stood his ground facing the hissing reptile's fangs, then took a swift swipe at the serpent's head while holding a protective paw to its nose. Mami recognised the cat's innate ability to know that the only vulnerable part of its body unprotected by fur was its nose. Another scary incident also involving a snake was the discovery of a large one hibernating in their prized horsehair settee. In the *bazaar* a shocked upholsterer, to whom the settee had been sent for repair, was confronted by a large curled reptile hibernating among the springs and wadding of this settee when he turned it over to inspect its underside. On hindsight, it was recalled that uneven lumps had been felt every time someone had sat down on that piece of furniture. The fact that these lumps seemed to 'disappear' if one thumped them hard enough had not been remarked upon at the time!

The sister nearest in age to Mami was Zari, a beautiful child with light hair and the much-prized slanting almond-shaped eyes. But Zari was a rebel, prone to disobedience, and she often got Mami into trouble along with herself. *Aghayé Doktor* was extremely strict with his daughters, and especially vigilant since Reza Shah's edict on modernisation meant that all girls should go to school. School uniform was the ubiquitous *sarafan,* a type of pinafore which could be worn over clothing. Zari would secretly sew up the hem of her *sarafan* to make it shorter, and loathing the regulation plaits with central parting, she often put her hair up in rag curlers at night. Mami never forgot the morning their father caught sight of them leaving for school with Zari's ringlets bobbing from beneath her headscarf. He strode out into the yard, pulled Zari up by her collar, turned her upside down in his strong arms and dunked her headfirst into the courtyard pool, then set her back on her feet with her hair hanging in wet strands from beneath her soaked headscarf. 'Never let me see either of you marching off like that all dolled up—or I'll forbid you to attend school!' Mami always complied with the strict code of conduct expected of them, but Zari, ever the rebel, often baulked at imposed restrictions. As matters transpired she would eventually escape as soon as possible into a loveless match that freed her from parental restraint, but not, unfortunately, from paternalistic restrictions that would follow her into married life.

~~~❧~~~

Mami's youth was spent in the eye of Reza Shah's cultural reforms and the one which affected women most was the abolition of the veil. Unlike Arab women Persian women have never hidden their faces. They have traditionally worn a garment known as the *châdor*. The word literally means 'tent'. In the military lingua franca of the Persian Empire soldiers were organised into *urdus* ('camps') where they were protected from the elements by pitching a *châdor* ('tent'). The term *châdor* also came to signify a protective tentlike covering for women. In essence the *châdor* is a large rectangle of thin cotton worn over the head and draped round the body. It cannot really be fixed onto the wearer other than by holding it together under the chin with one hand, thereby further restricting its wearer. Securing it with pins is considered to be both unsightly and defeatist. In negative terms the *châdor* relegates women to amorphous creatures. Young girls were taught to wear the *châdor* every time they left the house, even if they were only going out to play. They quickly became adept at holding on to it, though not much else could really be carried in the remaining free hand. Women are sometimes obliged to hold the ends of their *châdor* between their teeth when crossing a busy street simply in order to be able to carry a child in addition to a shopping bag. The *châdor* by virtue of its shapelessness and restriction has come to symbolise second-class citizen status for women, and 'ditching one's *châdor'* was taken as a sign of women's liberation. Reza Shah's reforms in the 1930s included a general ban of the *châdor*, and he paraded his own royal women in public without *châdors* wearing hats and *farangi* clothes. Religious people considered this to be scandalous and certain sectors of society refused to comply. In public places such as *bazaars* soldiers were posted to enforce the new rule and instructed to divest any woman of the offending garment and to cut it up with scissors, much like Russian soldiers in the time of Peter the Great who were equipped with shears to remove the long beards of the Boyars. Reza Shah's attempts to drag his demurring country firmly into the modern world were only partly successful, though like Peter the Great he is credited with creating the dawn of a more enlightened nation.

Mami's mother, always respectfully known as *Khânum Bozorg* ('Great Lady'), once had a humiliating experience involving the new *châdor* policy. One sweltering hot midday she realised that she had forgotten to buy bread. As her servant was busy in the kitchen, she lifted her purse, donned her shoes, grabbed her *châdor* and ran up the alley across the road to the local corner shop. Unfortunately, positioned in the doorway was an anti-*châdor* soldier keen for action. *Khânum Bozorg* was petrified as she had done what some women did in the midday heat—she had shed most of her clothes in the house and was clad only in a thin shift and her underwear. Thinking she would be up the street and back home in a jiffy she was semi-naked under her *châdor*. The soldier approached demanding that she hand over the garment. 'Rules are rules,' he said. 'Now give it to me.' *Khânum Bozorg* pleaded unavailingly. The soldier became impatient and yanked the outer edge of her *châdor* while she held on to its opposite edge in a grim tug of war. Before the soldier could win, *Khânum Bozorg* managed to break free and run back home clutching her modesty round her with both hands with her purse between her teeth, having left her new shoes behind in the scuffle. 'It is much better to lose one's shoes,' she said, 'than to lose one's *âberu* ('dignity').' The irony of this incident is that half a century later, following the

Islamic Revolution, Iranian women like *Khânum Bozorg* who had been in the vanguard of modernisation, and who had been persuaded to adopt Western style clothing, were forced back into the ungainly tentlike garment in the interests of the new Islamic modesty. Officials implementing this return to the dark ages were called known as the *monkerât* or 'purity police'. My grandmother, by then well into her nineties, was obliged to readapt and readopt the now loathsome garment. This was surely a sign that the world was coming to an end. 'No, it's a Revolution,' one of her sons informed her grimly, 'Revolution actually means "Everything Must Turn Around"!'

When Mami was about thirteen years old World War II began. Iran was a neutral country, though this fact was largely ignored by the Allies. Mami remembers bombers flying over Tehran. *Aghayé Doktor* had instructed that all of his children were to shelter in the *zir-zameen* or underground room if any planes were in the skies overhead. An illiterate woman servant called Naneh lived with them and helped to look after the children. On quite a few occasions Naneh coaxed her charges out of the safety of the *zir-zameen* and into the courtyard or the street to watch the circling aircraft. 'Come out, children, come out and see the big silver birds!' she would cry, and Mami and her brothers and sisters would tumble outside and stare open-mouthed at the Russian and British aircraft flying overhead.

❦

Mami's older brother Hushang was awarded a scholarship from the Shah's government to further his studies in Europe, in Birmingham as an engineering student. When Mami finished school she became a secretary and shorthand typist in one of the offices of the new Ministry of Health. There she met the young personable Dr Hafezi (Baba) who had been educated in England at University College Hospital in London. Their acquaintance was formal and relatively brief. Dr Hafezi was about to return to London to study further at the prestigious London School of Hygiene and Tropical Medicine. Mami said that she, too, was going to England. As the baby of the family Mami had enjoyed a greater degree of freedom than her brothers and sisters and there were few objections when she wanted to travel abroad, the main proviso being that she must be chaperoned by her brother. So in the summer of 1947 Mami and Hushang left Iran and travelled to England together.

They went north to Birmingham where Hushang was to study civil engineering. After a few weeks Mami enrolled as a Pupil Nurse in Birmingham's Dudley Road Hospital where she would live in the Nurses' Home and train for a diploma leading to qualification as a State Enrolled Nurse. While in training she would be provided with lodgings and a living wage. It seemed an opportunity too good to be true for a foreign girl—except that Mami grew homesick. She had never been away from home, had very little English and no friends. Her initial dreams of a wonderful life in *Farang* took a rapid nosedive in post-war Birmingham. She came to loathe the daily fare of boiled cabbage and lumpy semolina, the constantly grey skies, the gloomy industrial midlands, and the loneliness of her dormitory where cheery nurses were continuously slamming their doors and shouting *'Ta-raa, luv!'* Mami endured a few weeks of this life before telling her brother that she wasn't staying. Meanwhile, Hushang was happy in his digs, doing well in his studies, and had already met Margaret, the local English girl whom he eventually marry. He asked Mami to give it six months—if she didn't like it come next summer, he would take her home to Iran. Fate intervened. At some point during those six months, Baba, now a fully qualified doctor and a public health specialist, travelled to Birmingham to visit friends. He and Mami met once more, and this time a romance blossomed between them.

❦

At the close of 1946, funded by the new Shah's government, Baba had sailed to the United States to learn about sanitation in the

American prison service with a view to instituting similar measures in Iran. When he returned to London at the inception of Beveridge's new welfare state and Bevan's National Health Service it was to a city shrouded in a thick pea-soup fog where people queued on wet pavements clutching meagre ration coupons. Before leaving to go home he decided to go north to Birmingham to visit a number of his Iranian friends. There he and Mami met again. He was forty-two years old, and Mami was only twenty-five. While he was there they heard that Baba had been successful in gaining an appointment as a delegate for the Eastern Mediterranean Region at the International Health Organisation. This important organisation had been formed from the League of Nations, and a year later it was renamed the World Health Organisation, and became a branch of the new United Nations. Its headquarters were in Geneva, Switzerland, and it was a prestigious appointment. Baba wasted no time in asking Mami to marry him and move with him to Geneva. Mami loved Baba and readily agreed—marriage would also conveniently provide her with a welcome escape from Birmingham.

Baba and Mami, Geneva, 1950

Always one to do the right thing, Baba first returned to Iran to bid goodbye to his family in Semnan, and while there he went to ask *Khânum Bozorg* in Tehran for her daughter's hand in marriage. By then *Aghayé Doktor* was long dead, and Mami's mother was only too glad to see her youngest married off to this well-educated doctor—never mind that they would be living half-way round the world. All her other daughters already had several children, and Mami wasn't getting any younger—in fact, she was getting close to the age where she might already be thought of in traditional circles as *torshideh* ('soured') i.e., 'on the shelf'.

~~~❦~~~

In 1948 Baba and Mami tied the knot in a Birmingham registry office. Mami's brother, Hushang, and his new English wife, Margaret, were witnesses to the marriage. Baba and Mami never talked about this momentous occasion, and sadly no photographs were taken. Nevertheless it would have been a happy event. Mami cheerfully informed the formidable Matron in charge of the Nurses' Home that she was leaving Dudley Road Hospital for ever, an interview which she said mollified the stern lady when she also deposited on her desk more than twenty butter ration coupons which she had saved up in a drawer.

Baba and Mami travelled from Birmingham to Geneva at the close of 1949. They lived initially in a single room in the leafy suburb of Miremont, but soon moved to a modest flat with two bedrooms on the fifth floor of a residential apartment block in the Champel area. They would rent this flat for the next seventeen years, and it would become my childhood home. 'If only we had known we would live in *Farang* for so many years,' Mami would sigh, 'we could have saved up to buy it, and we would now be rich.' That flat definitely appreciated in value and would have been worth a small fortune by the time they eventually left Switzerland for Iran in 1965. But because they always knew they would one day return 'Home', and not sure exactly when that would be, they continued to pay rent year after year.

With Baba, Mami, and Lilli outside my childhood home in Geneva

Chapter 2

CHILDHOOD MEMORIES

The address *12 Chemin Thury, Champel* is indelibly imprinted in my mind. I lived here throughout my childhood, not far from the banks of the river Arve, tributary of the majestic Rhône in Geneva, Switzerland. Our apartment was on the top floor of a residential block at the terminus of bus number 33. I can see it now in my mind's eye—a white stone building five storeys high, with neat green retractable window awnings and rectangular balconies with matching green iron parapets. Ours was the middle in a block of three, each alliteratively named for a bird. No.12 was *Le Pinson* (the chaffinch), while on either side, if I remember rightly, were *Le Pic* (the magpie) and *Le Paôn* (the peacock). Further down the street were similar residential blocks: *l'Alouette*, *l'Hirondelle* and *le Cèdre*. I arrived here when I was just a few weeks old in the spring of 1950 from my parents' first home in nearby Miremont, and this was where we lived until I was fifteen years old. Our apartment was on the fifth floor. It was accessed by a polished stone staircase, though there was also a lift which in its day was considered to be the height of sophistication. We children were not allowed to use it unaccompanied, but we rode it frequently behind the backs of grown-ups.

At the front of the building was a wide pavement that lent itself admirably to our chalk drawings, hopscotch, endless ball games, and roller skating. In the centre was a small landscaped area with young sapling trees which were handy for securing the ends of our skipping ropes. All the children from neighbouring apartments played here on this wide pavement. It was a wonderful playground and we never lacked for companions. Along the back of the entire block ran a rough tarmac lane leading to a row of garages. This lane was little more than a gravel track full of potholes which regularly filled with rainwater. These potholes became for us a source of imaginary sea battles, shipwrecks and naval exploration which we would enact with boats fashioned from bits of newspaper and bridges made of matchsticks. Even more excitingly, the linked garage rooftops could be accessed by the more intrepid climbers amongst us, giving rise to a number of daredevil exploits. 'Going on the Garage Roof' was for us a significant dare.

At either end of this back lane the municipality had erected parallel iron bars designed to hang carpets ready for dust-beating. Once a month, our mothers would lug their rolled-up rugs downstairs to this area. With their hair wrapped in coloured kerchiefs they would proceed to thrash them with cane beaters. In-between times these iron bars became our jungle gym where we all practised somersaults, hanging upside-down from the uppermost bar by the crooks of our knees, trying not to display our underwear to passersby, letting go at the very last minute, and landing on the palms of our hands to the general applause and admiration of our peers.

A narrow staircase led from the top floor of our block to an attic area under the rafters. Each apartment was allocated a small lock-up which was their particular *grenier.* Ours was dusty, dark and cobwebby. Old suitcases bulging with what looked like untold treasures were stacked untidily in the corner and there was always a pervasive smell of dry wood and naphtha mothballs. When Mami went up there to collect something, my sister and I would follow—I loved its mystery. Behind a stack of dusty old vinyl records we discovered a battered suitcase with the gold initials 'H.H.' for Baba's name. This suitcase contained boxes of oblong, fragile glass slides akin to thin transparent dominoes. Under each slide were the remains of exotic creepy-crawlies, unusual larvae and long-legged mosquitoes. Each slide had been carefully labelled in indelible black ink with interesting names like 'Anopheles', 'Yellow Fever', 'Trypanosoma'. It was virtually an entire glass public health library. We spent many hours playing with them, lining them up like soldiers and trying to match the insects according to the span of their delicate wings.

Another section of the attic housed the *buanderie* or communal laundry. In the 1950s laundry was still mostly done entirely by hand. Every apartment in the block was allocated a day in the laundry area, following which the entire length of the rafters beneath the wooden eaves would be hung with damp washing. Our wash day was Tuesday and before we were old enough to go to school my sister and I would accompany Mami upstairs every week to the *buanderie*. I remember the strong smell of carbolic soap and the large metal cauldron in which Mami boiled our sheets and Baba's shirts, manfully stirring its steaming depths with a long wooden paddle. Other items were scrubbed energetically on the communal glass washboard. The whole process would take an entire day. I loved washdays; we could run races in the attic area, peer through the slatted gates of other residents' *greniers*, and play hide-and-seek between the wet sheets pegged to dry beneath the rafters.

Every apartment in our block was also allocated a small cellar storeroom underground in an area aptly named *la cave*. The very word worried us children. It was a low-ceilinged, damp, prison-like area, eerily lit by a single naked twenty-watt bulb. The contents of all the other *cave* storerooms were visible as their entrances were merely barred gates. Some peoples' *caves* were orderly with tidily stacked skis and other paraphernalia. Ours was a jumble of tin trunks, two broken chairs and a wooden sledge. We never lingered here—it was said to be inhabited by ghosts.

Baba and Mami created a traditional Persian home in our Swiss apartment. It was a cultural bubble at odds with its surroundings. Keeping one's heritage alive is now both expected and commonplace in immigrant homes, greatly adding to the diversity of community life, but in the 1950s we stuck out a mile as the foreigners—namely, *les étrangers*. We didn't mind this epithet, but we did resent the occasional inaccurate label of *les arabes*.

Baba's place of work was the impressive *Palais des Nations* on the other side of town. He left for work early every morning but always came home in his lunch hour, then returned to work in the afternoon. Mami would prepare a Persian meal for the whole family every single day. How she managed to acquire all the spices and herbs necessary for these feasts was a mystery, and doubtless the legacy of the constant stream of visitors from Iran who, over the years, enjoyed my parents' hospitality. Throughout my childhood we had a hot meal which consisted of a traditional Persian stew—a *khoresht*—every single lunchtime. My sister and I were expected to come home from school for it in order to eat *en famille,* and then to return for the afternoon session. Our school run involved a bus and two tram rides. Hence, every single weekday in term time we were obliged to ride twelve busses and trams to and from school! Our school lunch break was exactly one hour and forty minutes, just long enough for us to sit down for a plateful of rice and *khoresht,* with Baba and Mami, then sprint for the first tram back to school. We sometimes envied our classmates who were allowed to bring packets of sandwiches wrapped in greaseproof paper to school, as they were allowed to scoff their lunch and run out to the playground and let off steam before lessons. The only variable to our routine was the stew that Mami produced—every day was different, and we each had our favourite. I loved Wednesdays because it was *khoreshte bademjan* (lamb, tomatoes and aubergine with saffron), and I loathed Fridays because the menu invariably consisted of a concoction of leftover meat, often cooked with celery and prunes.

～❦～

When we were of an age to start school, Baba and Mami first considered the option of sending us to the local Swiss elementary school which was virtually on our doorstep, but decided against it when they realised we would be the only two foreign children attending the reception classes. Algeria was at that time in the news for gaining its independence, and they feared we might be looked upon mistakenly as *les petites arabes* (there is nothing more annoying to Iranians than being labelled 'Arab', though no Iranian would have dared to stick their neck out and explain that actually they were not Arab but Aryan). In the end they decided to send us to Ecolint, the *avant-garde* International School of Geneva where at least we would be among other non-Swiss nationals — never mind that all tuition would be in English.

Left to right, back row: Mami, Baba, Aunt Mehri; front row: Lilli, Farifteh

On a September morning, aged five, I was taken by Mami to the entrance of a low white building with the words 'Primary School' painted over the entrance in large letters. Wearing a gingham dress and squeaky patent leather shoes, I lined up in the yard with the other youngest pupils. On my back I proudly carried a satchel of the attaché case type which I would surreptitiously open just to inhale its heavenly smell of brand new leather. All around me children were chattering away in English — a language I didn't understand. As we waited in single file for our names to be called, one frightened child was physically sick, and was promptly removed from the line-up. The rest of us were marched into our new classroom and told to sit at a desk. The desks, each with its own inkwell, were arranged four to a row and painted a light green. We were then each given a small wooden-framed slate and a stick of white chalk which were to be our writing implements for the first term. So began my education.

I remember little of those first few months at Ecolint, except that I was unable to understand anything that was said to me, and I struggled for weeks to make myself understood. Nobody seemed overly concerned—certainly neither my teacher, nor my parents—I was just left to get on with it. And little by little the fog lifted, and by the end of the first term I emerged so completely fluent in English that I was given a speaking part in the class Nativity play! I cannot actually recall learning this language—I seem to have always known it. Neither has being thrown in at the deep end resulted in any adverse psychological effects. I actually blossomed in primary school, loved spelling, reading and comprehension but was no good at sums.

One particular incident stands out in my early school memories as a big childhood disappointment. It happened when I was eight years old. Each class was doing a little presentation at the end-of-year school show to which all parents were invited, and my class had a musical number involving the seasons. We were divided into four groups, each representing a different season, and told to get our mothers to turn us out in the appropriate representative colour for our costume. Spring Blossoms were to be dressed in pink, Summer Sunbeams in yellow, Autumn Leaves in brown, and Winter Snowflakes in white. I was a Snowflake and my group were the best dancers in the whole class. 'Any white dress will do,' said the teacher, reminding us of our costumes a week beforehand. I went home with a heavy heart that day, because I didn't have a white dress, though I secretly hoped that Mami might miraculously produce something—perhaps from bed sheets. But on this occasion Mami couldn't work any miracles. She said so emphatically. I had a red party dress which I could wear with white socks and shoes. 'It will be very nice,' she said.

'But Mami,' I wailed, in mounting panic, 'Snow is white, not red! All the snowflakes have to be dressed in white.'

'Well, you will just have to be a very special snowflake,' countered Mami crossly. 'It won't matter a bit; the dance will be lovely just the same, and in any case you'll stand out better from the crowd.' And that was the end of the conversation.

The following day I crept into school dressed in my now loathsome red party dress. All my classmates were assembled excitedly in the wings. The Sunbeams sparkled in their yellow dresses, the Autumn Leaves looked suitably drab in brown, and the lucky Blossoms were enchanting in pink. My worst fears were confirmed when I saw all the Snowflakes wearing pretty white dresses or white shirts with white shorts. When they caught sight of me they pointed and screamed with laughter. 'Look at Farifteh, Teacher! She can't be a Snowflake! Her dress is red!'

'My mother said I could be a special snowflake,' I pleaded. They sniggered, and I hung my head in shame. Of course I knew that red snowflakes didn't exist. Even Teacher agreed, and I knew I was defeated—I had known it all along, no matter what Mami said. While my ego was partly soothed by Teacher allowing me to become one of the two stage-hand curtain-pullers, the remaining Snowflakes went ahead on stage dancing the quadrille one person short. I watched them enviously, not caring. The unfairness of that incident still rankles to this day. It brought home to me for the first time that life could be unpredictable, and that grown-ups were not necessarily the demigods I had always presumed they were.

⚜

My sister and I were taught the Persian alphabet from an early age, and also the rudiments of reading and writing Persian (*Farsi*) by Mami. She also taught us the pillars of the Islamic faith, how to recite the standard prayers in Arabic which had to be memorised, how to perform the necessary ablutions, how to pray facing Mecca, and how to don a *châdor* properly. These 'lessons' always took place after we had done our homework at the end of the school day. School finished at half past four in the afternoon, and we invariably had to hurry home on public transport in order to have time to complete our homework. Since supper was at six, with bed and lights out at 8pm, this extra session always ate massively into our day. Eventually were able to rattle off the Arabic prayers which we learned by rote with some facility but with very little understanding. Mami and Baba were good Muslims, but not overtly devout. Baba privately had Sufi leanings, but he never discussed his beliefs with us. Mami did everything by the book, and this meant bringing up her children in the true faith. Perhaps she, too, balked at this additional burden to her day, but in the end she was glad that she had done her duty. I hated these prayer sessions—religion seemingly left me cold. Perhaps they sowed deep within me early seeds of seeking elsewhere the fulfilment of a longed-for spiritual dimension.

Near our apartment block was a children's playground where we were often taken by Mami on nice afternoons to play with other children on the slide, see-saw and jungle gym. It was also a great place for games of hide-and-seek among the pine trees that bordered the street, and, best of all, there was a marble drinking fountain with a brass spout from which ran a continual stream of pure crystalline water. We children always placed our mouths over the spout and stuck our tongues inside it to drink, and it was possibly the conduit for many of our childhood illnesses. One afternoon when I was about ten years old, I was playing in the park with my shiny new red ball, when something happened that awakened a deep longing within me. Clutching the ball under my arm I left the sandpit where I was playing and told Mami who was sitting on a park bench nearby that I was going to the fountain to get a drink of water.

As I bent my head upside down over the fountain and stuck my tongue into its brass spout, I could see across the quiet road to the entrance porch of the Catholic church of Sainte Thérèse on the opposite side. I had passed this building many times on our way to the park but hadn't taken much notice of it. Roman Catholicism was not on my radar. Even at my young age, I was aware that Geneva was an all-important seat of the Protestant faith, and our class had been taken to view the giant figures of the fathers of Calvinism carved from stone on the Reformation Wall of the University. Calvin, Knox, Beza and Farel were there, along with Coligny, Cromwell and a number of other dissenting worthies. Catholic churches weren't common in our area—there were several *temples protestants* dotted about district of Champel, but the *Eglise de Sainte Thérèse* was the only Catholic church in the locality. As I leaned over to take another sip, I saw that the church's doors were wide open, and in the distance twinkled what appeared to be little fairy lights. Curiosity emboldened me. Although I knew I wasn't allowed to cross the road, I did so, beckoned by those dancing lights. Peering nervously through the open doorway I perceived serried ranks of votive candles on a metal stand, their delicate flames flickering enticingly in the surrounding gloom. Stepping further into the building I seemingly entered another world. From somewhere in the depths of the cool dark building I heard male voices intoning *'Ave Maria, gratia plena...'* in Latin—this being an era still pre-Vatican II (the 1962 Council which modernised the Catholic Church). A nun with a magnificently starched winged headdress sat near the front, and a few grey women with headscarves were dotted around the polished pews. A young priest in a long black soutane glided noiselessly past me down the aisle and stopped to genuflect at the altar. No one paid the slightest attention to me—the kid with scuffed shoes, muddy knees and short skirt, clutching her ball. I stood open-mouthed, staring mutely at the numerous gilded icons and statues of saints, and the twelve impressively carved wooden Stations of the Cross hanging between the glorious stained glass windows through which streamed shafts of golden sunlight. Time stood still, and all noises seemed to evaporate in the distance. I felt drawn as if by an invisible magnet to this wonderful, intensely shimmering world. Somehow I knew with unerring certainty that this was a place where Kindness lived. As I stood rooted in its midst the wings of the stone angels seemed to bend low to envelop me with a gentle love. It was a defining moment in my young life—

a distinct epiphany—and I knew that I would return. I'm not exactly sure how long I stood there—perhaps not very long. Soon the real world re-emerged, and I could hear again birds singing outside and children playing in the distance. I retraced my steps, crossed the little road back to the park and took another sip of cold water from the fountain. 'Where on earth have you been?' scolded Mami. She could not know what I had experienced in the building that housed statues of 'infidels', and somehow I could not bring myself to tell her. I knew I had entered a sacred place where all is always well—the Secret World of God—where Love beckons to each one of us. And I knew that for the rest of my days I would seek it.

When I was old enough I moved up to Ecolint's Secondary School. From being happy and doing reasonably well, I started to feel less confident here where there was fierce competition not only in academic ability but also for looks and popularity. I was particularly bad at sports, and Physical Education became my least favourite subject. Each week the entire roll of girls from my form would assemble in a corner of the playing field and leaders would be appointed and made to pick their teams. Because of my seeming inability ever to win a race and a distinctly poor aim with balls, I was invariably among the last to be picked. I can still remember the shame of having to wait with the pitiful handful of girls who among us were either too fat, too dumpy, or self-acknowledged weaklings, while our athletic 'leaders' whispered amongst themselves about which team would have to be landed on this occasion with one of us 'undesirables'.

Then there was Latin. To my great chagrin I wasn't in the Latin class. Parents had been asked whether they wanted their children to take Latin in addition to the French and German taught in Swiss schools. We may not have had that choice in an ordinary grammar school, but ours was a progressive school where even half a century ago the governors recognised that not all its pupils were of European or American heritage, and that all might not necessarily benefit unequivocally from learning Latin — allowing for cultural diversity was obviously one of the school's strengths. Nevertheless, in the 'Latin or no Latin' stakes, the result was two classes of pupils taking Latin, which included all the brightest pupils in the year, and one class of all the remainder who were to do Typing. I really wanted to learn Latin — all my friends were doing it and I loved languages. The Typing class appeared to be full of kids who always struggled with their lessons and who were uncharitably labelled 'dimwits'. I didn't consider myself a dimwit. Baba reasoned that Typing was a skill that every girl should acquire, and Mami herself had been an able typist and adept at Pitman's Shorthand. Learning a living language was acceptable, but Latin was a dead language which no one spoke, so what reason was there to learn it? Had the choice been Arabic, for instance, they might have conceded as it was useful for Persian, but in this case there were to be no arguments — so to Typing I was duly sent. Once I was able to shrug off the fact that I was in a class with academically less able kids, I actually began to enjoy it — Typing was fun. We learned on massive, heavy, old-fashioned machines that had to be fetched from and returned to the shelves of a cupboard where they were always to be neatly stacked — an ordeal which ate up a quarter of our lesson time. Each pupil worked independently from a typing manual. I can still remember typing CCC/CAT/BBB/BAT, etc... Once we had reached a certain level of proficiency the teacher tested us by placing opaque white caps on each of our keyboard letters. Then, with a clock set to ring after exactly one minute we were to type 'blind', so to speak, as much of the page of a book in front of us, and as fast as we were able. After sixty seconds the bell would ring and we had to stop typing and count all the *correctly spelled* words — this was our final WPM or official 'words per minute score'. I learned to touch-type with ten fingers and eventually became quite proficient. I must admit that it is the single useful practical skill I have retained from my school days — one which I use every day on a computer keyboard. So perhaps Baba was right after all—though I still regret missing out on Latin.

Once a week we had Domestic Art. All the girls in the secondary school were taught sewing while the boys were marched off to do woodwork in the carpentry workshop. We went upstairs to the school loft where the sewing room was located. There we were taught how to hem handkerchiefs and blankets, each of which required a different type of stitch, and also how to smock and embroider. One day, our teacher got delivery of a large box which contained a special item. It was a new electric iron. Irons were expensive items and our mothers had mostly old-fashioned ones—Mami's old one had to be heated up on a stove. We were informed that our school was very fortunate to have been given such an expensive gift, and we were enjoined to take great care of it. Unfortunately, one day this iron slipped from my hands, and fell to the floor with an almighty clatter, emitting blue sparks. There was a sharp collective intake of breath as it lay broken on its side. Everyone stopped talking and covered their mouths in consternation. I promptly burst into tears. Wringing my hands pathetically I sobbed and sobbed and would not be comforted. Gathering up the broken iron and placing it on a shelf out of reach, the sewing teacher sat me down on a chair beside her and told me to dry my eyes. Her words still ring true today: 'No need to cry over a broken iron—there will be far more important things in life to cry over.'

~∞~

I think the most important advantage of my English language schooling was the fact that I became fluent in three languages from an early age. Lilli and I always spoke Persian at home, French in the street, and English at school, I have managed to retain reasonable conversational fluency in French and Persian, though I really consider English to be my 'mother tongue'. In my teens I was a voracious reader of books. As Baba and Mami's mother tongue wasn't English they didn't guide my reading in any way. I was left free to choose whatever I wanted to read from the school library and I literally read everything I could lay my hands on. At one stage I was reading more than ten books every week. I devoured most of the children's adventure stories then on the shelves: the *Secret Seven, Hardy Boys,* and *Nancy Drew* mysteries; the adventures of the *Bobbsey Twins,* as well as all Enid Blyton's story books of children's adventures in the English countryside, and stirring stories about life at boarding school. I also read many French books, especially the now dated books by Comtesse de Ségur such as *Les Malheurs de Sophie* with their wonderful illustrations of young demoiselles in crinolines and lacy underskirts. These were only the beginning of a lifelong love affair with books. My very favourites were those by C.S. Lewis, E. Nesbit, and Noel Streatfield, which I read over and over again. I loved E. Nesbit's three books in the *Psamméad* series: *Five Children and It, The Phoenix and the Carpet,* and *The Story of the Amulet,* all the books by Noel Streatfield, especially *Ballet Shoes, Tennis Shoes,* and *White Boots.* And I think I could recite all seven of C.S. Lewis's allegorical *Narnia* books almost by memory. I promised myself that I would read a 'proper' book every week, and for many years I did so. By the time I had left school I was familiar with most of the English classics. I wonder whether that would be true in today's age of television and other digital distractions—perhaps I was fortunate that Baba and Mami couldn't afford a TV.

***

I became a teenager in the 'sixties. To quote Dickens, 'It was the best of times, it was the worst of times....' (*A Tale of Two Cities*). It was certainly a bewildering time for our parents' generation as the well-ordered world which they had safely brought through the post-war years appeared slowly to disintegrate before their eyes. The world was shocked by the assassinations of President John Kennedy, Robert Kennedy and Martin Luther King; members of a new band called the Beatles became pop icons; and the hippy movement took off in America. Oddly enough, it was the unimportant details that seemed to bother grown-ups most. When the Beatles stopped over in Geneva on their way to Germany, they disrupted the city's airport which became the scene of an invading horde of screaming girls all appearing to swoon at the sight of the Fab Four. Parents were vociferous in their disapproval of such behaviour and the insidious negative influence of the Beatles with their haircuts and tight trousers. You would have thought the world was coming to an end the way grown-ups went on and on about it. Looking back at the snapshots I'm struck by how actually conservative the Beatles looked then—with just a short forelock, and wearing suits and ties, for goodness' sake! Baba had bought a new record player to replace our old phonograph with its brass wind-up handle, and with pocket money I was able to save up enough to purchase the Single 'Love, love me do' by the Beatles at 45 RPM, and I played it over and over again while I was doing my homework, much to his and Mami's annoyance.

With my sister Lilli in Geneva (I am on the right)

When I was fourteen, I bought my very first pair of tights from a department store in downtown Geneva. They were by a designer called Mary Quant and were made of a new stretchy material called *collants mousse* in French. Only available in large stores such as Uniprix, you couldn't buy them at the local mercer's outlet where Mami did most of her drapery shopping. Until then, before the arrival of tights, whenever we girls were allowed to ditch socks and wear 'nylons' for special occasions, we had to make do with seamed stockings held up by a garter belt and suspender. They never fitted properly—if you pulled them up too taut they might split at the knee when you sat down, and if you slackened them too much they would invariably wrinkle at the ankle. Women of my generation rarely appreciate the current vogue for 'sexy garters'. We loathed our cumbersome garter belts and celebrated the coming of tights as the greatest invention since sliced bread. Garter belts had four suspenders with metal hourglass-shaped hooks, each linked to a ceramic or rubber button designed to connect with the stocking and hold it up. The metal hooks would eventually begin to rust in the laundry, and the buttons would occasionally fall off without warning. This once happened to me as I was sitting in a tram—I felt a sudden sharp 'ping' beneath my skirt and when I stood up, the top of my stocking hung down one leg to just above the knee, mercifully still under my skirt. We got adept at improvising on the loss of these buttons—the best ruse was to use a small Swiss *five centime* coin as an emergency replacement, but failing that, an aspirin tablet would also do the job! After such battles, nothing can induce any one of us to reconsider the so-called 'glamour' of the garter belt.

On the other hand, bra-burning and 'flower power' were different matters altogether. Even I conceded they were a step too far. At home Baba and Mami explained that this was the danger of Western culture which had nothing in common with our decent Persian one. That's why they insisted on bringing us up properly with solid moral values. They were having none of the 'sixties freedom. They also knew that we would not live in Switzerland for ever as Baba's retirement was looming—but for now they had to keep their daughters safe from the temptations of bad *farangi* influences. I was fifteen years old when Baba turned sixty and retired from the World Health Organisation. He and Mami set their faces eastward, and were finally able to make good a promise they had made to themselves nearly twenty years earlier when they had married in Birmingham: 'When we retire we'll go back home to our roots.'

So at the age of fifteen, just when my world was opening up with a myriad of enticing prospects, I was obliged to leave behind the only life and home I had known. Baba and Mami were Going Home; but as far as I was concerned I would be going to a strange country, a new school, a different culture. And I wasn't happy.

University students meet the Shah and Empress Farah, Tehran
(I am 2nd from the left)

Chapter 3

IN THE SHADOW OF THE SHAHS

We arrived in Tehran in the autumn of 1965, a middle class Iranian family back from a lengthy *farangi* sojourn. Two years previously Mohamad Reza Shah, last sovereign of the Pahlavi dynasty, had instituted an acclaimed package of liberal reforms in Iran known as the 'White Revolution'. This included further land reforms, the privatisation of factories, voting rights for women, and an innovative literacy corps designed to work in conjunction with national service in rural areas. However, the gradual mechanisation of agriculture meant that less farm work was generally available and the population in cities like Tehran started to swell as dislocated families settled on its edges in what often became little more than shantytowns. While Iran began to enjoy a massive economic boom with the success of its oil revenues, and educated middle class families like Baba's and Mami's began to prosper, the latent dissatisfaction which simmered among farmers and labourers was largely obscured by the shiny veneer of 'progress'.

I was not aware of any ripples of social unrest or political dissent. In fact, Baba and Mami constantly marvelled at the transformation of the buzzing metropolis that Tehran had now become from the urban backwater they remembered. During the years he had worked for World Health Organisation Baba had been granted several subsidised 'Home Leave' breaks, but because international air travel to the Middle East was then such a major undertaking we had only visited Iran twice as a family during all those years. I remember those visits as an endless round of family parties in various houses, where legions of children were introduced as my cousins. My sister Lilli and I were paraded among this throng as celebrities, and some of our boorish *farangi* ways, such as plumping ourselves down in the best armchairs or interrupting adult conversation, were tolerated with condescending smiles. That tolerance changed, however, when we came to Iran for good. At fifteen I was considered virtually a grown-up. Mami often said that younger girls than me were already mothers themselves and capable of looking after entire households on their own. I was summarily expected to adopt Persian manners and observe the status quo. I tried to imagine what it would have been like if we hadn't come to Iran. I was already aware of having acquired a double identity, the product of two worlds—a European one which encouraged independence, and the Persian one of subservience to authority. This double identity became rooted within in my psyche, but I did wish I hadn't been forced into the mould of a half-baked *farangi*. I longed to be able to slot neatly and inconspicuously into a single culture. In time I would become an apologetic European in Iran, and an apologetic foreigner in Europe.

⁓⋇⋆⋇⁓

When we first arrived in Tehran we stayed with Mami's eldest sister, my Aunt Alam, in Mami's childhood home at the bottom of an alley in the downtown area of the city. Her elderly mother, *Khânum Bozorg*, still lived there. My parents' first job was to find a suitable family home. Eventually Baba found a modern house in the district of Yusefabad. It had a yard the size of a postage stamp with a pool whose length only allowed a swimmer three breast strokes from one end to the other, and it was unfortunately overlooked on all sides by tall buildings. Like many new homes springing up in the capital, it was billed for sale as 'Built by an Architect for Himself'. With four bedrooms, a roomy kitchen, and even a *zir-zameen* (basement room) Mami loved it instantly. When Baba went to complete the purchase he was told to wear clothing that would accommodate a stash of banknotes. Cheques were easy to forge and therefore not legal tender—at that time all business in Iran was transacted in hard cash. On the appointed day Lilli and I giggled helplessly at the sight of Baba emerging from the bedroom looking like a Michelin Man, having stuffed wads of money inside his shirt and trousers. Mami was cross: 'You wouldn't think it funny if your father was mugged in the street, would you?' she admonished sternly. A protective posse of relatives accompanied Baba to the Public Notary's Office where he safely, but somewhat less discreetly, divested himself of the cache. After the deeds had been signed, everyone returned to Aunt Alam's to toast the success of the purchase with tea and *bâghlavâ*. We moved in to our new home in the autumn of 1965, and my parents continued to live there for over a quarter of a century until Baba's death in 1992.

~~~❧~~~

The school year had already begun when we arrived in Tehran in the autumn of 1965. The problem for my sister and me was that the two schools that could have provided a relatively seamless transfer were deemed unsuitable. The British School only took pupils up to the age of fourteen which was the age when most British expatriates sent their offspring away to boarding schools in the United Kingdom. The American School did take pupils right up to senior school level with the American College Board as an exit examination. However, at that time many of my parents' friends held the partly misguided view that College Board exams were not on a par with the Iranian School Certificate by virtue of being taken at an earlier age, so the American School option was vetoed by Baba and Mami. Unfortunately, neither Lilli nor I possessed adequate written Persian language skills to enable us to attend a local Iranian senior school. In the end, our parents turned their attention to the next best solution: French schools.

We were first sent to an all-girls' convent school run by French nuns of the Order of St Vincent de Paul—the Jeanne d'Arc School of Tehran—which had a reputation for turning out accomplished *jeunes filles*. However, it transpired that its senior curriculum also ended at the tenth grade at which point most pupils transferred to the Lycée Razi' (named for Rhazes, the famed Persian scientist/philosopher). The Lycée was a mixed senior school preparing pupils for the Persian School Certificate in French. After a month with the nuns we were moved to this Lycée. My first year there was dire. Of two possible study streams—Literary and Scientific—I was interested only in the former, but not having previously studied either Persian or French Literature, this avenue was not possible. Instead, I was encouraged to struggle through the scientific curriculum—and *in French*!

The Lycée was situated in a poor district of Tehran. What had in previous times been a generously proportioned and elegantly colonnaded *maktab* was now a crumbling building with dusty windows and peeling stucco walls. New premises were in the process of being built uptown which would be a vast improvement. The original school had two segregated yards—a large one with a concrete basketball court for the boys, and a smaller one for girls. The link between the two was via a narrow, dark mud-and-straw tunnel. The girls' yard had a shack with an old flat-topped paraffin stove around which we girls crowded in the winter months to warm our hands, and where on arrival in the mornings we all parked our three-tiered aluminium dinner pails. By lunch-time the bottom tier containing *khoresht* ('stew') was piping hot, the middle container of rice reasonably warm, and the top receptacle containing either an orange or a few medlars just tepid. There was a single outdoor toilet in a lean-to hut for the entire roll of girls. After recess we were made to wait in single file in the mud tunnel while the boys were marched into class. Then, at a given signal, we filed silently past them to our seats. Each classroom held about forty pupils—twenty-five boys and fifteen girls. We sat on backless benches, three to a wooden desk. Being a late arrival I was placed in the very back row. Suffice it to say that I learnt very little during that first year except survival techniques such as inordinate amounts of copying and rote learning. My sister Lilli who was two years younger wasn't at the same crucial stage in terms of education and she was able to fit in much better, eventually becoming completely fluent in written Persian—something I have never been able to achieve.

I loathed the Lycée and struggled with all aspects of the scientific curriculum; but complaining got me nowhere—I was expected just to get on with it. I found mathematics particularly difficult, and it didn't do my confidence any favours to be told that all clever people are good at sums, by which comment I deduced that I must be a dullard. As I was on the verge of failing maths, Uncle Hushang, now a manager in the National Iranian Oil Company, was drafted in by Mami to tutor me at home. I remember enduring many a tear-stained session with the ever-patient Uncle Hushy, trying to understand the intricacies of logarithms and fractions while Mami hovered anxiously in the background. Somewhat miraculously, three years after arriving in Iran, I managed to limp ignominiously through the School Certificate exams and gain the coveted exit diploma which was my passport to the future.

<hr />

Life for us in 1960s Tehran was centred on our extended family and the observance of age-old Persian traditions rooted in the seasons. Tehran is five thousand feet above sea level and in winter snowfalls can be severe. Schools were often closed for a week during the winter term. On those occasions we would sit at home to sew or do homework. Many intrepid *farangi* Iranians went skiing in the mountain slopes north of Tehran, and although our family had learned to ski in Switzerland we never skied in Iran—at his age Baba was too cautious to negotiate the hazardous driving conditions in the mountains. Winter's main event for us was *Chaharshanbeh Suri* or 'Fire Wednesday', an ancient Zoroastrian custom of leaping over a row of burning bushes on the final Wednesday of the Persian solar year. Dried thorn bushes would be gathered beforehand and a series of little bonfires created in single file, often on the pavement right outside peoples' homes. At nightfall entire households would line up to hop over them while asking the Fire for its restorative properties by chanting a popular ditty, roughly translated as:

Bestow on me your rosy colour
And drive away my sickly pallor.

The Zoroastrian religion celebrates the triumph of light over darkness. Fire is revered as one of four sacred elements, representing goodness, light, and well-being. Unlike its Arab neighbours, Iran retained many ancient Zoroastrian traditions after adopting Islam, and the faithful observance of these traditions over many centuries has ensured the survival of Persian culture as unique among Islamic nations. Lilli and I were allowed to go unsupervised onto the street to jump over the line of fires, but we were banned from joining the crowds who followed this up with *ghâshogh-zani* ('spoon-beating') a custom which Baba deemed unseemly for his daughters to participate in: groups of people touring the streets dressed in shrouds to see out the evil spirits of the old year, banging spoons against pots and asking for them to be filled with treats. Hallowe'en is probably a *farangi* variant of this night.

The arrival of spring heralded another important Zoroastrian festival—the traditional Persian New Year or *Now-ruz*. Iran has preserved its ancient Persian solar calendar, and the first day of spring is New Year's Day—as it was in Roman times. *Now-ruz* is celebrated in Iran at the vernal equinox, and is the country's main annual feast or *Eid*. It is heralded well beforehand by assiduous spring-cleaning or *khâneh takâni* ('house shaking'). In every household the *Now-ruz* table or *sofreh* is given pride of place. This table contains an arrangement of seven symbolic items whose names all begin with the Persian letter *seen* (S). This is called the *Haft Seen*—or the 'Seven Ss'. These items are usually the following: *somâgh* (sumac), *serkeh* (vinegar), *senjed* (dried lotus), *samanu* (a sweet pudding), *sabzi* (sprouting greens), *seeb* (apple), and *seer* (garlic). The table also contains coloured eggs (a symbol of fertility), goldfish (symbolic of life), and a candle (symbolic of light), as well as a glass bowl filled with water containing an orange, representing the planet Earth. This orange is purported to turn on its axis at very moment of the vernal equinox, and children watch it like hawks every year hoping to catch this phenomenon—once or twice even Lilli and I thought we saw it move imperceptibly. As at Persian weddings, a large mirror is also placed on the table in order to capture reflections of the general joyous atmosphere. Unlike the Western New Year which is fixed at midnight, the actual time of the start of spring varies according to the exact moment when the sun reaches the equinox. This is always dictated by astronomy and is broadcast on the national news as a specific time, such as 11:27 or 15:23. At that precise moment Baba would be ready with a copy of the family Koran which he would hold aloft, leaving the house and shutting the gate firmly behind him. No one was allowed to enter until after he had rung the doorbell and been admitted. Thus the Koran, God's Holy Word, was given pre-eminence by being welcomed into our home before anyone else on the first day of every new year.

The giving and receiving of gifts at New Year followed two broad rules: elders gave to those younger than themselves, and the gifts were generally newly minted coins. This meant that family elders invariably gave gifts to everyone but received none themselves, while the youngest child gave no gifts but received from everyone. People had to work out who expected a present from them and how much they might expect to garner from older family members. If your parents were friendly with a rich family, you might even be given a gold *Pahlavi*—a coin specially minted during the Shah's reign, roughly equivalent to what used to be a British sovereign. *Half-Pahlavis* and *quarter-Pahlavis* were also available. Heads of family queued at banks in the week before *Now-ruz* exchanging old worn banknotes for crisp new ones and shiny coins specially minted for the occasion. Baba was well-organised and kept a stash of these in small box in a drawer of the wardrobe among his cufflinks and old-fashioned detachable collars. As a family elder he was expected to present coins not only to his own children but also to the offspring of all his various relatives. Children would have their purses with them at all times during the festive fortnight. You never knew who might call round and present you with new money.

Everyone also got new clothes at *Now-ruz*. Traditionally *Eid* clothes were made by dressmakers and tailors who worked feverishly day and night for weeks to benefit from this annual bonanza. As budding teens Lilli and I were allowed to choose the style we wanted. It was always a heart-stopping moment going with Mami to the local dressmaker with our roughly pencilled diagrams. Once there we could choose our fabric from the available range in the shop. Mami was careful with money and she would invariably downgrade our choice of expensive materials to a more workaday one. Once we had agreed on the design, the dressmaker would take crude measurements and vaguely estimate our proportions—we always feared she had got them wrong, but cannily the dresses always fitted perfectly. Our worst moment came when Mami started to haggle over the bill, which invariably culminated in her walking away saying it was ridiculously high, while Lilli and I ran pleadingly behind her. Eventually she would return, and after a further embarrassing discussion about inflation and how much cheaper the same stuff was three doors away in another shop, a final price would be agreed upon and we could breathe easy again. This rigmarole was repeated every year without fail. When Tehran's first department store opened in 1970, for the first time we were allowed to choose a shop-made outfit for *Now-ruz*. I loved my first off-the-peg dress even though Mami tut-tutted about the shoddy workmanship of the mass-produced garment.

Now-ruz lasts for twelve days and culminates on the thirteenth day in a mass picnic—the previously mentioned *Seezdah bé-dar* or 'Thirteen-Outdoors'. Iranians consider the number thirteen to be a bad omen. (An alternative translation of *bé-dar* is 'be gone!') For twelve days we visited friends and relatives, or friends and relatives visited us. An unwritten protocol was that family elders stayed put and everybody visited them first before going on to other relatives. The *Eid* visit itself ran according to an unvaried schedule. After a lot of kissing and polite admiration of the *Haft Seen*, tea would be served in small glasses with little sweetmeats. This would be followed in sequence by a glass of sherbet, trays of sliced fruit, little cakes, nuts, and more tea. It was important to judge the time spent at each venue carefully—too long would count as 'overstay' and too short would appear discourteous. Often, when it became difficult to cut the conversation and depart, one would be 'saved' by the sound of the doorbell ringing to announce another visiting party. This meant that we could politely say goodbye and move on to our next visit, though on the way out one had to greet the incoming party properly too—more kissing and politeness. One also had to be presentable at all times in case anybody called. Visitors never rang beforehand to say when, or even if, they were coming, but being caught unawares or unready was considered bad manners and poor housekeeping. Persian etiquette which always honours the guest as its central tenet ensures that no guest should ever feel that the visit has been ill-timed. *Now-ruz* is a hugely anticipated event in Iran, but the endless hospitality could sometimes take its toll.

❦

Summers are extremely hot in Tehran. Families who could afford to do so often took a holiday on the shores of the Caspian Sea in the northern province of Mazandaran. This was universally known as going to *Shomâl* ('The North'). Baba had distant Semnani relatives who sometimes rented a house on the beach in the summer and we would be invited to spend a week there. We loved holidays in *Shomâl*. It would take us several hours by car to drive through the Alborz mountain range that stretches between Tehran and the Caspian Sea. At first the scenery was dry scrubland. Then slowly we would start climbing the mountainous roads, carefully negotiating its many hairpin bends. Near the top we would stop in a small village called *Gach-Sar* where a teahouse served ice-cold *doogh* (a fizzy yoghurt drink) and refreshing slices of watermelon. Then the road would wind down into the deeply forested slopes that always took one's breath away. Rocky outcrops and desert thorns gave way to lush carpets of greenery, tea groves, and terraced paddies. We would wind down the car windows to smell the balmy air fragrant with the scent of young rice shoots. All along the roadside we would glimpse barefoot lads hawking punnets of sour berries and roasted ears of corn. Their cries of *'Tameshk!'* ('blackberries') and *'Balâl!'* ('corn') followed us on the wind as we sped past. Before long our noses would pick up the salty tang of the sea and we knew we were nearing the end of our journey. The beach house itself was mostly devoid of furniture, but relatives would arrive with massive Persian carpets rolled up on their car roofs to spread over the stone floors. Everything took place on these carpets—it is where we all sat to eat round a spread tablecloth, and also where we all slept on haphazardly laid cotton mattresses. In the morning all the children would run from the house down to the beach to paddle and swim in the warm shallow waters of the Caspian Sea. Sometimes if we were very lucky, a local fisherman might call round selling tiny amounts of fresh caviar in small plastic bags—probably contraband, as caviar is a commodity strictly controlled by the government. The tastiest snack in the entire world is surely a hunk of fresh buttered *nân* with a smear of caviar! My memory of who was who among the variegated relatives at the Caspian Sea is hazy, and every year the people we met there seemed different, but they were all in some way connected to Baba and as such were 'family'. Holidays in *Shomâl* were special and their memory still lingers as the vestige of a golden time in the minds of all of us who were young in the last decade of the late Shah's reign. Now mostly a middle-aged diaspora scattered across continents, our conversations on social media are still sometimes prefaced by: '…do you remember that perfect summer in *Shomâl*…?'

The blistering dry heat of a Tehran summer lasts for months. It was made more tolerable by full use of a *zir-zameen* ('basement room') and air conditioning which in those far-off days was a basic large metal box known universally as a *koolair*. Most houses had *koolairs* appended like large oblong aluminium carbuncles onto an outside wall. During the day we lived in our *zir-zameem* where it was several degrees cooler. Nothing much happened in the middle of the day and the city only woke up fully in the early evening. In order to make hot nights more tolerable many city householders took to sleeping on their flat rooftops. We did the same—it was wonderful to lie under the stars fanned by sultry night breezes, even though you had to go to bed early because you would be wakened at sunrise. If you slept in, the sun would start beating down on you soon after dawn, and you could end up with sunstroke by breakfast. Entire families would decamp to their rooftops at night erecting a makeshift bedroom space and some even had rooftop shelters to store their bedding during the day. Our flat roof was accessed via a rickety metal fire escape at the side of the house. When summer arrived we would lug four folding metal camp beds up to the roof.

Sleeping outdoors involved taking action against the pesky *pasheh* ('mosquito'). These insects appeared at dusk from nowhere and, unless preventive measures were taken, could plague you to death by dawn. We all slept inside mosquito nets—the ubiquitous *pasheh-band*. All family members were responsible for their own *pasheh-band*. Mami got ours tinted in different colours so that it would be clearly visible which one belonged to whom. Baba's was white, Mami's yellow, mine was pink and Lilli's blue. The nets were secured on to the beds by pre-drilling a hole at either end of the bed frames and inserting a metal T bar into them over which the mosquito netting would be draped. One had to ensure that the edges of the net were securely folded under one's mattress before dusk and that no holes or openings were visible or mosquitoes would invariably find a way in. Bedding and nets couldn't be left out in the open during the day or they would gather dust and leaves. We would fold the mattresses by rolling them up on our camp beds during the day, and remove the nets altogether. Unwritten *pasheh-band* policy dictated that you looked after your own net. Most summer mornings one or either of us girls would be industriously mending ripped corners with sewing thread much like seamen repairing their fishing nets. Occasionally summer storms would slash the Tehran night sky waking us with fat raindrops plopping onto our heads as we slept. All over the various rooftops cries of *'Barân, Barân!'* ('rain, rain!') would invariably be heard as whole families gathered up all the bedding they could and decamped indoors to shelter before they got completely soaked. On such occasions Lilli and I would always end up being incapacitated by fits of giggles seeing Baba in his long johns and Mami with her hair in curlers and a hairnet clambering down the metal fire escape in the middle of the night, trailing bedsheets and mosquito nets behind them. Now that I am more or less as old as they were then, I don't think this was at all funny, and it was really bad of us to laugh, but such was the ignorance of youth.

~☙~

Autumn is a lovely time in Tehran with crisp, sunny days, azure blue skies and an abundance of fruits. We gorged on figs, grapes, melons and quince. Schools opened again after the long summer break, and early mornings would witness queues of spotlessly turned out, satchel-toting kids chattering excitedly at every bus stop. I finished my schooling in 1968 which was a year of seismic social and political changes across the globe, from anti-Vietnam war and civil rights movements in the United States to protests in Europe, and war and famine in Africa. The world was never quite the same again after that year.

Iran witnessed a huge economic boom, especially when the price of crude oil doubled after the Yom Kippur War. Tehran gradually became a strange place—acres of new concrete and a constant presence of Western influences such as American cars and Pepsi-Cola vied with the *châdors* on the streets and the call to prayer from minarets at dawn and dusk. We were fortunate to be living in relative comfort in a northern suburb, and the underlying political unrest which, on hindsight, simmered just below the surface did not affect us. Like many ordinary citizens at that time we had no proper concept of politics apart from what the media offered, and because the media was mostly censored, what we thought we knew was skewed.

With Lilli in Tehran (I am on the left)

I actually loved the new burgeoning cosmopolitan freedom which meant that I could meet friends in the liberal northern suburbs of the capital wearing a modest miniskirt and platform shoes. Young people in the new Iran had never had it so good. Unlike our parents we had greater freedom to mix and make friends. Open-minded parents didn't object much if we met in cafés downtown for chat and social interaction, so long as we were always in a large group and were clearly visible in a public area, even though such activities were still frowned upon by the majority of traditional families. My goals in life were to go university and perhaps to get married. It was understood that this life plan would also include being an exemplary Muslim and nursing my parents in their old age—neither of which I would actually achieve.

In 1968 I got a place to study English Language and Literature at the new National University of Iran situated high above Tehran in the foothills of the magnificent Alborz Mountains. At last I was able to indulge fully in what I really loved—English books and poetry. During this halcyon time I studied hard and made many friends. Because I was already fluent in English I couldn't really take any credit for being a 'top student', but after years of being at the bottom in many subjects at school I admit to basking rather unashamedly in the glow of this new status. Most of the girls in my year went on to marry and have children quite soon after taking their degrees, and the handful of boys who also studied English became teachers and heads of language schools. I sometimes wonder what they are all doing now, post-Revolution and well into middle age. The beginning of the end of the last Shah's reign, which coincided with my undergraduate years, was a heady time, but it would all change dramatically in 1979 when our lives would be disrupted by the Islamic Revolution and foreign language academics like me would be branded as decadent pro-Western bootlickers and bear the brunt of the ensuing Purges.

My parents valued education very highly and were determined that their daughters would go to university and even beyond; however, they also clung to the notion that a girl's ultimate goal is to marry and raise a family. During my four undergraduate years there appeared at home a sporadic trickle of potential suitors for Lilli's or my hand in marriage. These suitors were thinly disguised by Mami and Baba as 'visiting family friends'. We were not consulted, and although my parents were too enlightened to 'arrange' a marriage, like many parents they realised that finding suitable prospective grooms in their social *milieu* was not always easy. On such occasions we would be expected to greet the visitors wearing our nicest frocks, and to dispense tea in a modest manner, listening politely while Baba expounded our virtues, and the young man's parents talked at length of their son's educational and business achievements. We invariably saw through our parents' thinly veiled subterfuge and refused to bite any bullets. Indeed, after the 'visitors' had departed, Lilli and I would retreat upstairs to compare notes on this latest unfortunate suitor's less-than-perfect features, often consumed with embarrassed mirth at the thought that either of us might consider getting hitched—let alone to *him*!

With the Nassiris in Tehran (I am seated on the left;
Aghayé Senator and Amu-jan are standing 2ⁿᵈ and 3ʳᵈ from the left)

Among our parents' close friends there was one family whose friendship meant more than anything to Baba. These were the Nassiris from Baba's home town, Semnan. The two brothers who long ago along with Baba had received a prophecy from a soothsayer that each of them would go on to achieve great things were from this family. Each of the lads had indeed achieved much in life, just as the *rammâl* had prophesied. Baba who was told he would heal the sick became a doctor; the elder of the brothers who was told he would become 'close to the Sultan' was now a Member of Parliament; and the younger who would 'become a warrior and wield the sword' had risen to the rank of army general. The Nassiris were our closest friends, and the bonds between our families were almost like blood ties.

The younger of those brothers, General Nassiri, still a bachelor in his fifties, was known to us as *Amu-jan* ('Uncle dear'). He had a house with a magnificent swimming pool which we all enjoyed, and he was invariably a generous host. I remember being carried in his arms as a young child, fascinated by the row of medals on his rough serge army tunic. He and Baba could often be observed at family gatherings deep in conversation. We all knew that that *Amu-jan* had close personal ties with the Shah, but just accepted that the Shah was obviously close to all his generals. Occasionally we would hear snippets of political talk but none of us paid much attention—we were interested in more mundane matters such as investigating the crate of mangoes newly arrived from Pakistan that had been delivered to *Amu-jan's* mansion and which he proceeded to distribute among us, or the new Alsatian puppy that was being trained as his guard dog.

That *Amu-jan* had become indispensable to the Shah was clear after his appointment as the head of SAVAK—Iran's organisation for intelligence and national security—the secret police which protected the Shah's regime. We were largely unaware of SAVAK's activities, and certainly *Amu-jan*, who was always kind and loveable, never spoke about this aspect of his work. Like many ordinary citizens we were protected by a censored media which lauded the Shah as the country's saviour and spoon-fed us with sugary reports on modernisation and progress. In later years the political culture of the Shah's government became more repressive as well as more remote, and SAVAK's new target became the eradication of any fomenting radical movement. If one listened to

the late-night radio broadcasts on the BBC World Service, one became aware that terms such as 'torture' and 'Amnesty International' were increasingly being mentioned, though incredibly
many Iranians discounted such reports as evidence of the West's
envy of their country's progress! We remained largely cocooned
from rumblings of social unrest and insulated from the lives of
those less fortunate who eked a meagre existence in the slums on
the southern edges of the city. I vaguely remember Baba discuss-
ing the Shah's latest reforms with gentlemen friends who called
round for tea and Persian poetry readings, but I remained ignorant of the politics.

Outside our home in Tehran (I am wearing the uniform of the Lycée)

The National University of Iran where I was an undergraduate
was situated high in the Alborz foothills north of Tehran, in the
district of Evin. Sometimes during our lunch breaks when we
students sat outside in the sunshine eating our sandwiches, loud
banging and shouts could be heard in the distance accompanied

by the clanging of heavy iron gates. We knew that there was a prison in nearby Evin, and assumed that the noise must be from prison officers trying to park their vehicles in the gated compound. Not for one minute did any of us associate those ominous noises with nefarious activities. How naïve we all were! Looking back, decades later, I am convinced that terrible things did occur in that infamous prison whose name would not be long in becoming synonymous with torture and death. How is it that we did not understand that politics was morphing into a show of public sycophancy to the Shah, that the dichotomy between an educated minority and the illiterate masses had become too wide to bridge, or that the pull of fundamentalist Islam was far greater that anyone had assumed? What had once happened in France and in Russia was about to happen again. Iran's regime was slowly but inexorably ripening for a fall.

It was against this backdrop that I completed my honours degree and was awarded a First Class BA in English Studies.

University of Nottingham

Chapter 4

ACADEMIC INTERLUDE

I graduated in English Studies from Tehran's National University in 1972 with distinction. This wasn't too difficult because previous English schooling had ensured that my language skills were initially better than those of my fellow students. My aim now was to go to England and to study English literature properly. Nowadays university education is often seen as a rite of passage, a fruitful stage of development between adolescence and adulthood, in which fulfilment of latent talents and the exchange of ideas can take place. 'Enjoy your university years, you're only young once' is an oft-heard mantra. In Iran, as in other developing nations, such a premise is subordinate to the ultimate goal of further education which is academic excellence. Luckily for me, at that time furthering one's studies at a *farangi* establishment was considered to be a worthy aim. At twenty-two I was ready to leave home.

Mami was fifty years old, Baba nearly seventy, and my sister was at a local college training to become a social worker when I began applying to English universities. I first targeted the prestigious ones such as Oxford and Cambridge, sending each one a copy of my degree and an academic résumé. Receiving swift rejections from these establishments I began to look further afield. I spent virtually spent the entire summer mailing applications to British universities—I wasn't so keen on the United States, partly because of its geographic distance from Iran, and partly because I aspired to walk in the hallowed footsteps of Shakespeare, Milton and Wordsworth. Each separate application involved a laborious process of writing the introductory letter, completing the application form (being sure to retain carbon copies) and getting each packet weighed, recorded and mailed from Tehran's Central Post Office. After this there was usually a wait of two, sometimes even three, weeks for a postal reply. I didn't dare to send off too many at once in case I was inundated with offers of acceptance. That didn't happen—as it soon became abundantly clear. Nevertheless, my perseverance was finally rewarded when I eventually received a positive response from a red-brick university in the English Midlands. Nottingham offered to enrol me for the degree of MPhil by research in English Literature conditional to my proving academic capability during my first year, and subject to my being able to finance the overseas tuition fees. (At that time, these fees were considered shockingly expensive at £250 per annum!) My ecstasy knew no bounds as I ran to Baba waving the letter and dancing with joy.

However, there was something else to consider—something for which other students might have given their eye-teeth. In 1972 the National University of Iran had applied for funding on behalf of several of their most able students, including me, to study at the then prestigious American University of Beirut. I had been one of the few lucky students awarded a full two-year bursary, all expenses paid, to study English Language and Literature leading to a Master of Arts in English with a Diploma in Teaching English as a Foreign Language. Baba and Mami would thus be spared a financial burden, and on completion I would also be guaranteed a job of my choosing at any higher education establishment within Iran. It was a huge honour and a 'win-win' situation. I was left with no doubts that everyone considered me to be extremely fortunate.

Except that I didn't want to go to Beirut—I was desperate to go to England! Every atom of my body rebelled against studying English in yet another non-English-speaking country. What was the use of that? It would be like learning about the human brain by studying the anatomy of primates. But the offer from Nottingham University was less attractive than the one from Beirut— there were no guarantees that I would be able to continue there after one academic year, and I certainly wasn't provided with any financial incentives.

At home there ensued a fortnight of pleas and counter-pleas. Baba and Mami were conscious of the 'honour' that the scholarship provided, and were reluctant for me to reject it. They said it would be madness to forego such an amazing opportunity of free education in such a lovely city (at the time, Beirut had the soubriquet 'Riviera of the Middle East') with a job guarantee at the end of it. And moreover they worried that its rejection might be construed as a snub to the awarding authority. Iranians seem to harbour an inbred anxiety of going against any official authority. But I continued to plead, perhaps only half-aware of the burden which going so far from home far away to England, as opposed to half that distance away in the Levant might place on the family, and eventually Baba relented.

To his eternal credit, Baba said that he just wanted me to be happy. Maybe there was also an element of thinking that it was equally an honour to have been accepted by a *farangi* institution. Baba himself had aspired to go to England and had done well there. He managed to persuade Mami, who was always extra careful with money, that he could finance one academic year for me at Nottingham, and after that I would have to apply for a Shah's grant for study abroad. These financial incentives were only available to the very best students, so it would be incumbent upon me to excel in my first year. With the optimism of youth I joyfully agreed. (Interestingly, had I chosen to go to Beirut I could not have completed my studies there, as civil war broke out in 1975 and the university closed indefinitely.) My future began to look rosy, and I looked forward to it immensely, little aware of the mountain that I would need to climb. Because I had already lived in *Farang* I was supremely confident and felt no anxieties about going so far from home for such a long time.

The year 1972 was one of international disasters: the Munich Olympics ended in bloodshed for the Israeli team, the Watergate scandal erupted in the United States, and there was Bloody Sunday in Ireland. But that summer I felt the world was a wonderful place. I now marvel at the equanimity of my parents as I prepared to fly the proverbial nest. In days before the advent of the Internet and mobile phones, going abroad meant I would be well and truly gone for a whole year, and there would be no communication between us except via post. My air ticket was booked with the date of return set for the summer of the following year. Should I be obliged to phone home for any reason, I would need to book a call through the international 'carrier' from a main post office, and it would be up to me to synchronise the timed call with the time zone difference and the post office's opening hours. I once had to do this during my years at Nottingham, and it involved a cold pre-dawn wait outside their central post office in case I missed my international phone call slot which was booked to commence exactly two minutes after the post office opened. (Young people just don't know how easy they have these days!)

When I formally accepted Nottingham's offer, I was duly sent an Accommodation Pack which guaranteed me a room in a female Hall of Residence along with a list of necessary items such as towels, a mug, bedding, etc. Nowadays it's unthinkable that a student would need to factor all this extra stuff into a single suitcase for the aeroplane journey—one could just buy or borrow most of it locally on arrival. For some reason that course of action did not occur to us, and I spent hours trying to fit a year's worth of books, stationery, and clothes in my 20kg allocated luggage allowance. Among the suggested list of things to bring, which I treated as a list set in tablets of stone, was one item whose meaning eluded us. That item was 'tea towel'. What on earth was it? We searched fruitlessly in our dictionaries. The word did not appear under 'tea' neither was it listed under 'towel', and there were definitely no entries for 'tea towel'. I even resorted to asking a number of English teachers, most of whom were, it has to be said, elderly Iranians. No one seemed to know. So I had to complete my packing without the said item. That just showed the paltry level of familiarity with idiomatic English among our faculty staff—and it made me realise that being labelled 'top student of English' in my year really meant next to nothing.

Individuals leaving Iran had to submit their passport to the airline agency which had issued their travel documents two days prior to departure. Your passport would then be couriered to the airport on the day of departure and you would be able to pick it up after going through airport Security. If you got to Security and your passport was withheld it meant that you were *matrood*—i.e. barred from leaving the country—and this could be for a number of valid or fictitious reasons: political activism, owing money, incipient imprisonment, or even just 'irregularity' were the usual culprits. It was every passenger's nightmare that his or her passport would be withheld at the departure gate. This anxiety was made worse by the fact that you would not be forewarned, and therefore you were not only ready to travel, but you had already said your goodbyes and had even sometimes cleared Security before the Sword of Damocles descended. In those days—unlike a decade later—the sword did not fall too often, but it fell nevertheless fairly unpredictably. Baba said he had once seen a pickup truck outside the airline ticket office in downtown Tehran with the driver loading passports in the back ready to take to the airport for the next day, when he suddenly tripped, spilling a crate-load of passports onto the road. Though he hastened to pick them up and sped away through the traffic, Baba wondered what would happen to the passenger if one had been inadvertently missed in the gutter. Stories like this, magnified by rumour, were in the psyche of every Iranian traveller and didn't inspire confidence. It was only after securing their passport at the departure gate that passengers could finally relax and look forward to their journey.

After arriving at Heathrow I made my way to Nottingham University by train from the station at St Pancras. I still remember the names of the stations along the way: Bedford, Kettering, Market Harborough, Leicester, Loughborough. Nottingham was not a city anyone at home had heard much about, but I had done my research thoroughly and I knew it had been the heart of the lace-making industry, the original home of Boots the Chemist, and the manufacturing town for Raleigh bicycles and Players cigarettes. The university was fairly unique among the more recently established ones in that it was situated in a campus of parkland with a lake and twelve halls of residence dotted within its beautiful grounds. I arrived at Willoughby Hall one bright September afternoon, and when I saw the number of massive trunks piled up in the entrance hall I knew I needn't have worried about the size of my heavy suitcase! The atmosphere in the female dorm was quite jolly with girls running in and out of one another's rooms. I had been allocated study bedroom F16 which was the sixteenth room along F corridor on the fifth floor of the building. Each identical study bedroom was fitted with a desk, a bookcase jutting over the single bed (the bed was designed to turn into a settee during the day), a wardrobe and a wash basin. In all it was a cosy room with a view over a courtyard and the green fields of the Boots pharmaceutical experimental laboratories in the distance. I quickly unpacked and looked forward to life as a bona fide student. I considered myself quite worldly-wise, being a postgraduate and at least four years older than the innocent undergraduates with whom I was surrounded.

That premise was quickly proved wrong. I was naïve and innocent and completely unworldly-wise. In fact it would take me many months before I achieved even a modicum of independent confidence in student society. I had led a very sheltered life and although cerebral and reflective, I possessed very few practical skills. Having never lived away from home I would not have survived that first year in self-catering digs, so it was just as well that I had landed in catered accommodation.

On the first evening all the girls queued up outside the dining room waiting for the dinner bell. When the doors opened we trooped into the servery area where we collected our cutlery and a tray, and the serving staff handed us a plate of food which on that particular evening consisted of fish, peas, and mashed potatoes, along with a bowl of apple crumble. We then proceeded past a row of metal tanks from each of which protruded a long ladle. The tanks contained what looked like various sauces. I could see that the first one was full of ketchup, the one next to it was filled with a creamy white sauce, and the one at the end was full of a hot yellow sauce. I deduced that hot sauce must go with hot food, so I ladled the thick yellow liquid on my fish. The white sauce looked as if it might be a sort of gooseberry cream, so I poured that over my pudding. That was all wrong! I knew it as soon as I sat down and looked at everyone else's plate. What I had assumed was a hot hollandaise sauce was actually custard, and what I had taken for gooseberry cream was *sauce tartare*. Nevertheless, because I was from Iran, no way was I Going to Lose Face, so I ploughed gamely on and ate my horrible dinner without a murmur—an incident which always causes much hilarity whenever I recount it. And much as I loved my study bedroom, I thought it strange that one had to wedge oneself underneath the bookcase in order to be able to lie down in the bed. It took me several weeks of getting bruised every time I turned over in my sleep to realise that the narrow bench settee was designed to be pulled away from under the bookcase at night to convert it into a proper stand-alone bed!

⚜

My first meeting in the English Department was not a success. I had officially enrolled on the 'MPhil by Research' course. At my university in Iran 'doing research' meant going to the library and reading up on authors and poets in encyclopaedias, the Oxford Companion to Literature and other such tomes. When I first met my professor in Nottingham he asked whether I had a field of research in mind. I replied that I didn't—I had assumed that I would be somehow taken through the process, and that I would need at the very least to produce a few preliminary essays. But this professor merely waved his hand, saying succinctly:

'Go and read, then come back to see me in a few months—you may be onto something by then.'

I was horrified. 'Go and read *for a few months*?' What about lectures and tutorials? The bottom fell out of my world. Ever-

~ *81* ~

conscious that I needed to prove academic prowess by the end of my first year in order to get a grant from the government in Iran, and well aware that Baba was shelling out hard-earned cash to send me here, I was in a near panic, and quickly realised that I really didn't know the first thing about what I was supposed to be doing. Fortunately I had the temerity to say to the professor there and then that I thought I had made a mistake and had enrolled on the wrong course. The professor looked me up and down for a while in silence, stroking his grizzly beard. Finally he sighed, and said:

'I can only suggest that you give up the idea of an MPhil for now and enrol instead on the one-year course leading to a Diploma in English Studies for Overseas Students — it's designed to bring foreign students of English up to scratch.' If I did well enough, I could re-apply to begin the MPhil. This was a remedial option which would perforce put my plans back by a whole year, but it was a lifeline, and I took it. I thanked the professor with an embarrassing profusion of gratitude that only Iranians instilled in Persian etiquette can muster. 'No worries,' said the professor. 'And by the way, is it very hot in Baghdad?' I was at some pains to correct his hazy grasp of Middle East geography in the politest way possible!

The worst thing was writing an explanatory letter about this 'downgrade' to Baba and Mami outlining this change of plan, knowing that by the time it was delivered to our house in Iran, I would already be halfway through the first trimester of the Diploma. I am eternally grateful that my parents did not criticise me at that distance for this academic comedown — I don't think I could have endured reading letters containing 'what if...' scenarios — nor did they harp on the missed opportunity of the American University of Beirut whose prospectus was full of supportive lectures and tutorials. Baba must also have realised that he would have to finance an extra year abroad for me, but I heard no more about it. At last, I was free to experience pleasure in 'the groves of academe'.

Outside Willoughby Hall, Nottingham University

F Floor where my bedroom was situated at the all-girls Willoughby Hall became known as 'the Friendly Floor' because everyone billeted there was a new student and we all rapidly became good friends. The twenty single study-bedrooms were situated along a narrow corridor with their doors facing one another. Each was occupied by an undergraduate from a different part of the country and enrolled in a different university department—I was the only postgraduate among them and probably the oldest as well as the most naïve. But I was able to relate to all of them and many of us are still in touch with one another through social media half a century later. I think the single most influential factor in the formation of enduring friendships among this disparate collection of females in such a goldfish bowl setting was the fact that en suite facilities were completely non-existent. At one end of the corridor there was a row of three toilets and three adjoining bathrooms each containing an enormous bathtub—that was the sum of the facilities. Showers were an unknown phenomenon in these old residences. Several times per day we all met going to and from the washrooms. A good deal of jolly camaraderie ensued with the use of the baths. Girls would 'bag' a bathtub by running its taps and slinging a towel over the door, then sprint back along the corridor to collect their trusty 'trannie' (no student was without a cherished transistor radio—*the* techno equipment of the day). Three girls could take a bath simultaneously in adjoining bathrooms. It usually resulted with all three singing raucously at the top of their voices and cracking jokes over the flimsy partition walls, often joined by others who were visiting the facilities. *'Things happen after a BADEDAS bath'* read the label on our pricey bubble bath bottles depicting a towel-clad maiden with Rapunzel-like hair at a turret window looking down at her prince mounted on a white charger below. So we, too, dreamt of our future princes as we luxuriated in the fragrant depths of soapy BADEDAS bubbles. The very fact that we didn't have private washing facilities meant that we got to know one another pretty quickly and few of us felt lonely in this sisterhood on F Floor.

As soon as I had started on my new course I knew I would love it and I set out determined to study very hard. I knew I wasn't at Nottingham University to enjoy myself, but only to study and do well. Among the score or so of overseas students on the same course, I was academically fine and didn't find the work too exacting. It was fortunate that such a good solution had been available for me, and also that Nottingham was a 'campus university' with all the academic departments and university buildings on the same site in beautiful parkland. This was not always the case elsewhere, and I did hear sad tales of lonely, newly-arrived foreign students in similar situations to mine who found themselves having to negotiate complex daily treks to and from solitary suburban digs across city conurbations. By the end of the first trimester I knew I would be capable of continuing with literature research the following year. I started to relax and enjoy it all, and this involved making tentative forays into student life—albeit without the alcohol and sex which seemed to dominate the 'after-hours' scene.

One puzzling aspect of campus life was an almost prolific use of abbreviations. Conversations seemed to be sprinkled with them. For instance the student sitting room in Willoughby Hall was universally known as the JCR (Junior Common Room), not to be confused with the plusher senior one which was the SCR. The student union or SU was situated in PB (Portland Building), which also housed a bar known as the Buttery and was adjacent to the engineering departments of 'MekEnj' (mechanical engineering), 'CivEnj' (civil engineering) and 'KemEnj' (chemical engineering). Then there were the numerous student Societies known simply as SOC. So the main religious ones were: AngSoc, CathSoc, Meth-Soc, and the active ones: RamSoc (rambling), HocSoc (hockey), ClogSoc (folk dancing). There was a FrogSoc (French Society), and even a SocSoc (Social Society)! Various buildings and halls of residence were also known by time-hallowed abbreviations. Hence, one didn't refer to Portland Building, or Florence Boot Hall or Hugh Stewart Hall by their proper names—they were invariably called PB, FB, and HuStu. It took me, a self-confessed reasonable English linguist, several weeks to decipher the meaning of sentences like the following:

'Hiya, I'm off to PB after KemEnj class to have a roll and a skinful in the Buttery. Maybe see you at the ClogSoc knees-up? Oh, we're having a pow-wow with the Orienteers in FB/JCR later—see ya!'

'Don't you feel really safe here?' is a question I would some-times ask my friends. When asked why, I would always reply, 'Be-cause we're on an *island!*' I don't think it had occurred to any of them that they actually lived somewhere reasonably inviolable and unlikely to be threatened by turncoats or quislings residing on their country's borders. Iran currently shares its frontiers with eight different ethnic groups, all of which have their own separate agendas: Pakistan, Afghanistan, Turkmenistan, Azerbaijan, Armenia, Turkey, and Iraq, as well as nomadic Kurds in the northwest. The Persian Gulf and Arabian Sea in the south borders the neighbouring Arab Gulf states. Throughout the centuries Iran has had to redefine its boundaries depending on invasions from neighbouring peoples. Folk living on the opposite side of the arbitrary frontier lines are often sympathetic and even intermarry with those on The Other Side. When I was a student at Nottingham the north of Iran had 5,000 miles of common frontier with communist Soviet USSR. Being an island nation Great Britain doesn't have this problem, and I thought it was strange that people I spoke to had never thought of themselves as 'safe' in this respect.

～❦～

Willoughby Hall slowly began to feel like home for me. So much so, that at the end of the first trimester when the month-long Christmas break arrived I was in for a rude awakening. At Christmas the university virtually shut down and all the students and staff left to go home. There were always a few foreign students who stayed, but it was expected that most would be offered hospitality with friends, or decamp elsewhere off campus. Although I had made some friends, I didn't know anyone well enough at this stage to be invited to their homes for Christmas. I wasn't worried because we students were told that there would be one hall with a limited number of rooms kept open for students who had nowhere to go during the holidays. I assumed that, this being the Land of Plenty, we poor 'foreign-students-with-nowhere-to-go' were to be given a jolly good time in a student facility with turkey and all the trimmings laid on. I had seen illustrations in glossy periodicals of a typical Christmas dinner and knew that the British *Farangis* ate this sumptuous meal along with *flambéed* Christmas pudding, and pulled Christmas crackers. And if we were lucky enough, perhaps there would even be a Father Christmas lurking nearby with a sack full of useful little presents specially selected for us. I even had visions of rewarding with 'figgy pudding' the carol singers who would surely come to sing at our hostel on Christmas Eve. In fact I was really looking forward to my first *farangi* Christmas. I had planned to attend my very first Midnight Mass in the city centre, and was anticipating all the jollity that would ensue the next day.

My first shock was learning that I would have to move lock, stock, and barrel out of my cosy little study bedroom for the duration—and that meant moving everything out: bedding, crockery, books, framed photographs of my family, posters on the wall—the whole lot. The second shock was having nowhere to store it. For the next month Willoughby Hall would be a Conference venue for paying delegates. I had to budget spending some of my student grant to acquire two extra suitcases, packing them with all the belongings I could do without, and hire a taxi to take me to the railway station to park them in Left Luggage until next term. Another shock was seeing everyone around me waving goodbye and being collected by relatives on the final day of term. 'Have a great Christmas! See you in the New Year!' they shouted through their car windows as they drove away.

'Are you going to be OK?' someone from F Floor asked.

'Sure, I'm going to spend Christmas at Wortley Hall,' I answered. The very name 'Wortley Hall' sounded very grand, and I imagined it to be a house akin to the grandeur of Evelyn Waugh's Brideshead. The fact that other students didn't seem to think it was too fantastic a venue didn't really register. In any case, I had no other option.

When I arrived at Wortley Hall with my battered suitcase containing everything I would need for a month's vacation, I received the next, and probably biggest, shock. I was horrified to discover that Wortley was a long single storey prefabricated hut erected to billet airmen during the last war which had been put to use as the annexe to a nearby house. It was deemed unsuitable for the use of paying conference delegates during the university break, but suitable to house the cheaper alternative of overseas students who required holiday accommodation. Wortley Hall was a really just a long shed with dark cell-like rooms off its central corridor, each with a window that faced an outside brick wall. At one end of the corridor there was a tiny kitchen with a single ring Baby Belling electric stove and a small refrigerator, and at the other a bathroom with a stained old bathtub and two toilet cubicles. The room I had been allocated was in the middle of this corridor. On either side were two other females, like me, also holiday residents. One of them was a pretty Chinese girl called Eva whose Chinese boyfriend called often—they would cook noodles together on the stove and disappear into her bedroom to eat. I never saw Eva eating anything other than noodles. On the other side of me was an African girl whose room always teemed with noisy Africans who constantly talked and laughed at the top of their voices at all hours with the bedroom door open. There was no sitting room in the building. So you were basically stuck within your own four walls. Never mind, I thought, I'm going to spend all my time in the university library and really get on with my English essays. Nobody told me that the library would also be closed over the festive season. And then there was the shock of discovering that all shops, including grocery stores, closed for the holidays, too. In Iran nothing ever shut. In fact, shops did their best business during holidays and holy days. I was completely caught out at 4 pm on Christmas Eve when I realised that I couldn't buy anything—and I had not thought about food! Eva and her boyfriend had departed somewhere. The African contingent was engaged in the opprobrious activities such as endlessly swilling booze and smoking—in fact the whole corridor now reeked of rum, cigarette smoke and weed.

I was reasonably close to tears that first Christmas Eve when reality finally sank in. I was stuck in a prefab hut on the edge of a closed university campus with no food for the holiday weekend except one small tin of corned beef. I had no transport to go anywhere in town, and the buses weren't running. The library was shut, and all the shops had also shut early. Great! Outside a thick fog had descended, swirling round the windows, and though it was only late afternoon, darkness had already fallen. It was at that point that I made yet another horrible discovery—I didn't have a tin-opener! How on earth was I going to get at the corned beef? I ransacked the Wortley kitchenette, but all I found were a few plates, a ladle, and some plastic cutlery. Being reasonably hungry by this time, I went outside and found a sharp stone. I reckoned that the can of luncheon meat was probably made of quite thin aluminium and if I could just pierce a corner of it, I could probably wedge it open somehow. Perhaps I might even summon the courage to knock at the room next door and ask if one of the burly visiting African men might do it for me. It was while I was pounding away at the can with my rock that salvation arrived. An ordinary-looking man wearing a clerical collar and a university scarf put his head round my door. He had knocked but had received no answer. Amused by my hammering of the tin of beef, he said, 'Hello. I'm Stuart, the university's Methodist Chaplain. Just wondering whether you might like to go somewhere for Christmas lunch tomorrow? I'm also the minister of a church near the campus and a number of my parishioners are offering hospitality to overseas students...'

Would I? Hell, of course I would!

On Christmas morning in-between church services and his own family Christmas lunch, the Reverend Stuart Burgess came by car to collect me from Wortley Hall and delivered me to the home of one of the two elderly spinsters in his congregation, Elsie and Ivy, who took me in for the day and treated me with the utmost kindness and generosity. They were completely unfazed by the fact that I was not a Christian, and neither of them really knew where Iran was. To them I was just a student far from home and probably lonely, and they pulled out all the stops to make my first Christmas really special. Elsie and Ivy were neighbours and members of the nearby Methodist Church where the University

Methodist chaplain was also a team minister. They had worshipped there all their lives and neither had ever married—there just weren't enough men to go round after the end of the war, they said.

I remember that *farangi* Christmas clearly, perched politely on the shiny mock-leather settee in Elsie's parlour, where three ceramic flying ducks graced the wall over the fireplace and an *art deco* clock in a solid mahogany frame ticked loudly on the mantelpiece. A small electric heater in the corner of the room gave out a modicum of warmth. Ivy busied herself in the tiny kitchen and somehow managed to produce a celebratory meal of turkey, sprouts and potatoes, complete with a white sauce, incongruously called Bread Sauce (those sauces again!). We had sherry trifle for dessert and there was also a small Christmas pudding which Ivy had initially made, as is traditional, weeks previously on All-Hallow's Eve, and into the mixture of which she had added a single old silver sixpence. The two ladies made sure that it was my portion which contained the silver coin. When I surprisingly bit into it, they both clapped their hands with glee saying that good fortune would be my lot in the coming year. I was also given a small wrapped gift which turned out to be a scented bar of soap.

Elsie and Ivy asked about my family but also talked about their own lives which centred on the local Methodist Church. Elsie was involved with the Sunday school, and Ivy sang in its choir. They explained I would always be most welcome there, and that it was a church where lots of students came for the Sunday service, and significantly, that not all of them were Methodists—some weren't even Christians! Church isn't only about worship, they explained, but also about fellowship and friendship. That was a relatively new concept for me. I had always considered worship to be solely about a believer's intimate relationship with God—and about trying to live a sinless life and better oneself in His eyes by regular prayer. Somehow it hadn't occurred to me that it could also inform and enhance social interaction.

Reverend Stuart Burgess was a wonderful chaplain to the students, but he was also a great minister to all his other parishioners. They loved his inclusive ways and his unerring ability to see the wider picture in terms of worship and fellowship. Young people flocked to his church from all over town not only for worship but also for the coffee and chat afterwards. Stuart and his wife Elisabeth, along with their two young children, invited any students attending the Methodist Church Service on Sunday morning back to their home afterwards for coffee, biscuits, and a chat. This weekly occurrence provided students with a listening ear and a regular contact with normal family life. It was to become the focal point of my week for the remainder of my years at Nottingham. A whole new world opened up for me. Through the fellowship of that particular Methodist Church and the kindness of ordinary people like Elsie and Ivy, Stuart, Elisabeth and others who worshipped there I first came to really know Christ. It was the beginning of a lifelong love affair with Him and His Church—about which more later.

As an aside, I should mention that seven years and a whole lifetime later, back in Iran when it was in the grip of martial law and chaos reigned in Tehran during the Islamic Revolution, one day a letter was miraculously delivered to our house even though postal services had long been suspended. It was addressed to me in a shaky handwriting, and inside was a five pound banknote along with the message: 'Thinking of you at this difficult time— your friends, Elsie and Ivy.' The old two ladies must have been well into their eighties then, and the five pounds would have been frugally saved from their pensions. Sadly, when I finally eventually managed to get to Britain after the Revolution, Elsie was long dead, and Ivy was failing in a nursing home. I was never able to thank them personally for their generous gift, nor tell them how much their timely message had meant to me in those dark hours. I could only hope that somehow in an afterlife they were rewarded for their generosity to a student they had briefly befriended.

After my first year I flew home for the summer holidays and reassured Baba and Mami that I was happy at Nottingham University and also that I had now been accepted on a course leading to research, initially the MPhil, which would later be transferrable to PhD. Things had moved on at home. My younger sister was now married and expecting a baby — a first grandchild for Baba and Mami. Baba, though officially retired, had been persuaded to continue to give Public Health lectures to medical students at the National University in Tehran, a part-time work which he greatly enjoyed. There was also some initial pressure from well-meaning relatives for me to marry and settle down. I was aware of vague murmurings about the dangers of becoming a *torshideh* bluestocking — an overly-intellectual 'old maid' — a couple of my aunts were even dropping rather heavy-handed hints about eligible bachelors! I wasn't the least bit interested and put my foot firmly down. I insisted on finishing my studies, and my main let-out clause was that a well-educated bride would be eminently more desirable.

When I returned to Nottingham that autumn, I was fortunate to be chosen by the Rector of Willoughby Hall to become one of several 'Moral Tutors' there along with my friend Marion. This sinecure was a sought-after position among postgraduates. It involved my moving from F Floor into a one-bedroomed flatlet within the building in which I would be allowed to remain over the holidays, eliminating the need to remove myself and my belongings to Wortley or elsewhere. In return I would be responsible for the 'moral welfare', so to speak, of approximately twenty undergraduates. In reality this involved little more than making sure none of them was becoming depressed or suicidal, and that noise was kept to minimum after 10pm. It also involved inviting your group to your flat for a drink from time to time. As I was completely teetotal, I had to ask for lessons on serving sherry. Another duty was manning the fire escape exits once every term during a pre-dawn testing of the Hall fire alarm, and ticking off students' names as they emerged. The first folk bolting down those exit stairs were invariably men in various states of undress who quickly escaped round the back of the building. Again, this was a complete surprise to me—a 'moral tutor' so painfully naïve that I had never suspected such goings-on in an all-female dormitory.

Marion

During my second year I applied for, and was awarded, a bursary from the Shah's government, now rich with oil revenues. This gave me the financial assistance I needed for the next few years to complete my doctorate. On my return to Iran, I would need to pay this back by working as a university lecturer for double the number of years I had been sponsored. What more could any student wish for than financial security with the guarantee of a university lectureship in the Alma Mater? The only proviso was that nothing less than a PhD would be acceptable. Returning with an MPhil, for instance, would be viewed as a failure. The offer seemed almost too good to be true. I, along with many other Iranian students of my generation, blithely signed these lucrative contracts. We didn't look very closely at the small print which clearly stated that if for any reason we were unable to fulfil its stated conditions, we would be liable to a fine of 'a million times the value of the grant in the currency of the day' and, in addition, imprisonment for a 'betrayal of trust'. Even wise Baba said this was probably just an idle threat to ensure that a wholesale brain drain didn't occur in Iran. No one could have predicted the overthrow of the regime, but several years later, in the purges that followed political chaos, many university lecturers were illegally sacked by a kangaroo government which decided on the spot that neither they nor their post would be 'useful' to the new Islamic Republic, and I, along with many others like me, would potentially fall foul of this contract.

~━✦━~

I had finally got my PhD thesis on track. Its title was 'Faith and Doubt in Poets of the Nineteenth Century', a comparative study of the discrete modes in which six nineteenth-century poets approached religious belief, using its ambivalent issues of faith, doubt and compromise to explore the nature of teleological truths. The range of enquiry extended from the Romantic age to the modern period, and was extensive in order to show the poetic continuity of a whole century in terms of spiritual curiosity, involvement, and anxiety. I started with Keats whose anti-clerical reaction to the Christianity of his times established his interest in a philosophy of faith. My thesis then explored the poetic responses to faith and doubt in four Victorian poets (Tennyson, Browning, Arnold, and Clough), each of whom sought to expose the many facets of conflict in their minds between a traditional synthesis of Christian thought and the heterodoxy of 'honest doubt'. The final poet was another who, like Keats, had died young and was unpublished in his own lifetime—Gerard Manley Hopkins, a Jesuit, who was a man of faith in an age of doubt. I challenged the view that he forced secular themes into religious contexts, showing that his religious faith resulted in poems that are actually private prayers which evolved in composition through careful and conscientious craftsmanship. I was fortunate in having discovered unpublished material for this final section preserved among Hopkins' papers at the Bodleian Library in Oxford. My thesis also had a comprehensive summary of the ecclesiastical, theological and scientific upheavals of the Victorian age, covering areas of social tension and emphasising the dilemmas of religious conversion. I must admit, reading some of it now, the whole thing strikes me as major intellectual exercise, and indeed I spent four long years in an 'ivory tower' in order to accomplish it. The historical aspects led me to study English church history in detail and this involved a lot of reading in the Theology Department where, as a bona fide Muslim, I was a bit of an oddity.

This is where my supervisor stepped in with a suggestion. As a Muslim I couldn't possibly hope to understand the life of a Religious. Hopkins converted from high Anglicanism to Roman Catholicism in the wake of the nineteenth-century Oxford Movement and later became a Jesuit priest. In order to be able to write cogently and intelligently about him I would need to understand what underpins both monasticism and the life of a priestly scholar in Holy Orders. In order to gain this knowledge in as short a time as was possible, my supervisor's novel suggestion was: *'Get thee to a nunnery, go...!'* (Shakespeare, *Hamlet,* Act 3, Scene 1). Interesting fieldwork—the only problem was that I first had to get accepted by one!

I applied assiduously to countless convents up and down the country, asking to live in their community for a while. Most politely rejected me outright, and certainly none of the contemplative orders had a place for a Muslim student of English Literature wishing to research the monastic life. However, at long last I was rewarded by receiving a positive response from the Passionist

Sisters in Leeds. And that is where I took myself off to for a month in February 1975.

The Passionists are a Roman Catholic order of monks and nuns founded by Saint Paul of the Cross. They place a special emphasis on the Passion of Jesus Christ, seeking to unify their lives and apostolate with the Passion and keep alive its memory in daily life and work. Professed members of the Leeds convent were mainly teachers, but many were also involved in various social welfare projects. I was welcomed as a visitor and given a small bedroom on a corridor near other young nuns, most of whom went out to work every day. The Passionists are an 'open' order, and hence their rooms were not called 'cells'. They wore the habit, but as this was now post-Vatican II they had short veils and sensible skirts. The community took all its meals together, and they were allowed to talk, though after supper the Grand Silence was religiously observed until after breakfast the next morning. Several times during the day the Angelus would be rung, and anyone who was in the House would go to the Chapel for prayers. The convent was like a large family with a crowd of grown-up daughters. Their nuns were outgoing and always very friendly, and full of fun—not at all stuffy. One young Irish nun told me that when she entered the Order she was sent a list of clothing to bring, and her mother had taken her off to Dunnes and bought her outrageous psychedelic-patterned and leopard-spotted underwear.

'There might be a Rule about what you wear on the outside,' she said, 'but there ain't no rule 'bout yer knickers!' They were so completely 'normal' and unlike my mental image of what nuns were like. A few even went swimming once a week in the local baths.

'Swimming?' I asked. 'What about the habit and your veils?' 'Oh we just change quickly in a cubicle and put our uniforms inside a bag. No one can tell we're nuns when we're in our swimsuits.'

'Except,' interjected another, 'when we forget and shout "*Sister*, over here!" from across the pool!'

It was Mother Superior, Sister Gerard Majella CP, a wise woman, who decided that while I was with them I should also be introduced to an enclosed order. Not far from Leeds, near Wetherby, there was a contemplative order whose convent was simply called Carmel. This was a small community of Carmelite Nuns. The Carmelites are a Roman Catholic order whose members cultivate the contemplative life in all its aspects, leading a life of prayer solely within the confines of their community. We waited in Carmel's parlour, a large bare room cut completely into two halves by a metal grille which stretched the height of the entire room from floor to ceiling. Their Mother Superior presently appeared behind the grille, dressed in a flowing back habit and wearing sandals on her feet—hence their proper label of 'Discalced' Order of Carmelites. She was flanked by two Novices whose robes and veils were pure white. Mother Superior sat on a chair on the convent side of the grille, while we drew up chairs to face them on the 'world side'. She explained that the grille was not meant to shut out the world, but was a symbol to remind the contemplatives that they had chosen a life apart from the world.

'We don't have a TV but we listen to the news on the radio once a day, and from that we gain all the information we need for prayer,' she said. 'If you believe in the power of prayer, then this place is a powerhouse of prayer.'

Mother Superior also asked a lot about me, why I was with the Passionists, and what I was doing at university. She was genuinely interested, and did not give the impression that she had shut herself away merely to pray—she was very well informed about the world and a good conversationalist, despite the fact that Carmelites spend ninety-nine percent of their day in absolute silence. The Novices did not speak, but I felt they, too, were genuinely interested in the chat. When we rose to leave and Sister Gerard thanked Mother Superior, I said that perhaps one day I would like to return to pray in their chapel. That never happened, but I do believe that Mother Superior in the Wetherby Carmel prayed for my eventual conversion, and I so wish I could tell her that, although it took a long time, I finally 'Did It'. In a funny way, I think that maybe somehow she already knows.

I loved the Passionist Sisters and secretly envied their community and personal lives based on prayer and service. I wished I had been born a Christian, so that I could wholeheartedly embrace going to church as often as I liked without feeling guilty of a wholesale betrayal. The whole experience awakened in me a deep desire to connect more deeply to Jesus Christ as my personal saviour but I knew it was out of the question for now — but maybe, just perhaps maybe, sometime in the future? I dared to hope so.

More of this type of 'field work' about which Baba and Mami knew nothing followed a year later when I made the first of many visits to St Beuno's in North Wales. This was the Jesuit establishment where Gerard Manley Hopkins had completed the Theologate part of his training for the priesthood and where 'The Wreck of the Deutschland', 'God's Grandeur', 'The Windhover' and a number of his other famous poems had been written. It was the destination *par excellence* for students of Hopkins, and it did not disappoint.

The Jesuit House which I first visited in the 1970s was almost unchanged from Hopkins's day, and even now that it is a well-known Retreat centre run by Jesuits, it still has the same external appearance. Crucially, the beautiful rolling North Welsh countryside which so captivated and inspired Hopkins is still unspoilt. Getting to Tremeirchion from Nottingham involved changing trains at Crewe and taking the Welsh coastal line bound for Llandudno and Holyhead. In those days trains would stop at the small cathedral town of St Asaph, not far from Tremeirchion, but nowadays you need to disembark down on the coast at Rhyl. My experience of St Beuno's was yet another piece in the complex jigsaw which finally led me to become a Christian.

Once again, I was warmly welcomed by the resident Jesuit priests, and especially by Father Superior, Michael O'Halloran SJ;

and not a single priest or lay brother seemed the least bit concerned by the fact that I was a non-Christian female. I was given a study bedroom on the top floor, up a narrow wooden staircase in the wing under the roof, aptly named 'Attica'. As in Hopkins's time it looked out over fields dotted with lambs in springtime and stooks of wheat at harvest. From my window on a clear day I could just about make out the twin spires of the two cathedrals, one Anglican, one Catholic, across the Wirral peninsula in Liverpool. One of the best things that happened to me in the few weeks that I initially spent here was that I was allocated my very own 'guardian angel'—the name by which Jesuits appointed someone who knew the ropes to look after a newbie.

My 'guardian angel' was a white-haired, elderly Scot in a wheelchair. His name was Father Peter McIlhenny SJ. In every sense we were worlds apart. Yet, incongruous as it seemed, we hit it off—big time. Fr McIlhenny had a long-standing disability and had been wheelchair-bound for many years. However, he was also extremely learned, had been a Latin scholar, had studied at Campion Hall in Oxford, and worked in South Africa and previously at the Vatican. Originally from a small mining community in Lochgelly, Fife, he had left Scotland at an early age to join the Jesuits, and had at one time been the Novice Master in the Jesuit English Province. At the time we met, he had been living at St Beuno's for a number of years, as unlike many other old Jesuit houses, the dining room, chapel and the larger bedrooms of the main house were all situated along the same long corridor and easily wheelchair-accessible.

Father Peter became my unofficial mentor, and quite apart giving me sound advice on all sorts of things, he also translated parts of Thomas of Aquinas' 1485 *Summa Theologica* from Latin into English for me. Over the next few years, and right up until his death, he remained my most constant advisor, confessor, father substitute, and friend. He was probably the single most influential person in my struggle for Christ. Yes, he was a Jesuit, and yes, Jesuits are supposed to be subtly casuistic, but in reality I think that because he was a Jesuit and therefore not a monastic, and because of his extensive education (it takes many years to become a Jesuit priest) and his profound understanding not only of Ethics but also of the human condition, he was able to see 'the bigger picture' and to meet me on a level which gave me the confidence to proceed with my studies, steadied my mind, enriched my faith, and made me feel cherished. In this way he gently but surely was able to guide me finally into the arms of my Saviour. However, I digress, as I will say more about my conversion in a later chapter.

～✲～

As far as academic work was concerned, I worked hard, and after four years of supervised research and writing, I had almost completed my mammoth thesis which, because of its size, would need to be bound in two volumes. But first, my Bibliography and all the References, of which there were literally hundreds, which I had gathered over the course of four years' research, would have to be checked diligently for absolute accuracy. Nowadays, digital access to the Internet means that this is fairly straightforward and can be legitimately regarded as 'literary housekeeping'. Back in the mid-1970s this technology was still a long way off. Each cited book, periodical, and journal article had to be checked manually for accuracy of title, date of publication, and citation page numbers. In order to do this I was obliged to seek a national Legal Deposit library, and my decision rested on the famous Bodleian situated in Oxford, the town which Matthew Arnold had immortalised in his elegy *Thyrsis* as '…that sweet city with her dreaming spires'.

I decamped to a self-catering hostel in Oxford early in the new year of 1977 and paid to live there for three months. That particular winter was a severe one and my room was equipped with a single-bar heater which needed to be fed with coins, so the warm confines of a library proved very welcome. Every day I would trudge across a snowy common to the Bodleian's Reading Room. Students were allowed to request only six books to be fetched from the archives at any one time. I sat silently at a polished ma-hogany desk and listed the titles of the books or journals I needed on a square of vellum paper which I handed to a steward. He would take it with one hand and pad away silently, like a panther stalking prey, pulling on his white cotton gloves with the other. Approximately twenty minutes later he would re-emerge, gliding towards me just as silently as before, having either climbed a lad-der to reach the dizzying heights of the shelved upper echelons, or having descended down a spiral staircase into bowels of the building, but he always returned bearing the six requested vol-umes in his gloved hands. This laborious scenario was repeated request by request, day by day, and week by week, on and on and on, *ad nauseam*—until one day when the snow had melted and daffodils were appearing on the banks of the Cherwell, it was fi-nally finished. I had checked them all. It had taken me nearly three months, but I knew that all my References were now correct. Job done!

After that I got the thesis typed up by a university Science secretary who advertised her services on a notice board in the Students' Union. She typed dissertations for cash in the eve-ning on one of their large departmental typewriters. Her boss didn't mind as long as the paper and typewriter ribbons were paid for. Computers weren't in existence then and my mini portable typewriter from Woolworths wasn't up to the task. Considering that my two-volume PhD was over a thousand pages in length, she actually managed to buy a second-hand car with the proceeds! Getting the work typed and bound took at least two months. Three bound copies of the work had to be submitted. Until 1977 all English Department theses at Not-tingham University were carbon-copied, which meant each page was typed up with three sheets of paper interlaced with black carbon paper all inserted together into the typewriter in order to produce one fair copy and two carbon copies. If you were lucky, both carbon copies would be equally legible, though sometimes the last copy would be much fainter. It was the bane of the typists who had to strike the keys very firmly while typing, and in pre-Tippex days every error involved removing all three pages from the typewriter and gently scraping away at the error with a special abrasive octagonal eraser. If you rubbed too firmly, the paper could rip and there were invariably smudges on the two carbon copies. If the mistake involved a large chunk of writing, it was just easier to tear up the page and type it all over again. A computer programme's convenient 'Cut', 'Paste' and 'Backspace' options are truly gifts to any writer! My doctoral thesis was one of the first in our Department which was copied using a new mass-marketed machine called a 'Xerox' copier—prototype of the now familiar photocopier. This technology was so new that fellow students would come up to me and ask to see the end product.

'Are you really telling me that this page is the exact image of that page?' they would ask, reverently fingering the photocopied paper. People nowadays laugh when I recount this, but what is really laughable about it is that it didn't happen so long ago!

There were three of us foreign postgraduate students of English Literature working on doctoral theses at Nottingham during my years at the university. The other two postgraduates were further advanced in their studies. One was a Brazilian girl from Belo Horizonte and the other an Iraqi Christian girl from Mosul. Both students submitted their theses a few months before I was due to submit mine. When the time came for their viva voce examinations with an external examiner, it was extremely unfortunate that each of their theses was downgraded from PhD to a Masters degree. Both girls suffered near nervous breakdowns as a result, because like me they had been sponsored financially by their respective governments.

Such an unforeseen and irrevocable downgrading after several years of research is now much less common, as a dissertation which isn't up to scratch is usually deferred early on pending amendments. This was not necessarily the case forty years ago, and the thought of it put the fear of God into me. Ugly rumours were flying round the department about a 'clampdown on substandard submissions', especially by foreign students of English, to prevent lowering the standard of the top academic degrees. I was about to submit my thesis and I knew that, unless I returned to Iran with a piece of paper with 'PhD' clearly marked on it, my life would not be worth living. But I passed! It was the jubilant moment—the acme of academic aspiration!

❧

The Graduation Ceremony, where I sat in the front row, one of only a handful of graduands wearing the distinctive crimson robe and the circular hard hat that marked us 'Doctors' out as a higher species, felt nothing less than a sweet victory which I savoured to the full. Expensive international telephone communications between Nottingham and Tehran ensured that Baba and Mami could also revel in the success of their clever daughter, who against odds had achieved academic excellence in *Farang*. The following few days passed in a blur of happiness and graduation parties. Far from Nottingham, '… away in the loveable west', to quote my Jesuit poet Hopkins (*The Wreck of the Deutschland*), Father Peter McIlhenny SJ also gave thanks in the chapel at St Beuno's in his own private Mass. Everyone I knew rejoiced for me, but most of all, as I rejoiced for myself, I knew deep down that Someone greater than me had nudged, cajoled, and comforted me through the entire process, and in humble gratitude I could only kneel in reverent prayer: '…my Lord and my God!'

Beneath the outward exuberance, however, there was a gnawing sadness that my Academic Interlude was now at an end, my *farangi* adventure was at an end, and a love affair was also at an end…. Iran inexorably beckoned, and though I always knew that I would one day return—there was after all a debt to repay—it now felt as if I was facing a future without consolation. Why this sadness at such a happy time?

❧

Gentle Reader, I have not yet spoken about The Man. We had met in my final months at Nottingham University. I was in love, and the thought of losing this love so soon, wrenched from me by circumstances beyond my control, felt almost unbearable. I will tell you all about it in the following chapter.

James Robb (medical graduation, 1975)

LOVE

I was twenty-six years old when I first discovered love. Before that I thought I knew what love was, but I didn't—not really. It happened in my final year at Nottingham University. I was in the Theology department trying to get to grips with English ecclesiastical history, with one of the lecturers guiding me through the reading material. This was a very jolly Welshman who, in later years, would be appointed Professor of Theology at Durham University. Dr Douglas Davies was a larger-than-life character and always great fun to be with. No one was ever down in the dumps when he was around: his infectious laugh could often be heard resounding through the hushed sanctum of 'Theology'. Even the tidy departmental secretaries forgave his endlessly messy attempts at making tea and coffee in their tiny cubbyhole. He would happily inform you that he was engaged in research on the 'Mormons of Merthyr Tydfil', always adding with an impish chuckle—'all six of them!'

But behind the external bonhomie, Douglas was a serious academic and also an Anglican priest. We soon struck up an easy friendship, he and I, and in-between giving seminars and lectures he would pop into Theology's Reading Room to see how I was getting on. It was through him that I discovered such seminal texts as the *Apologia pro Vita Sua* of John Henry Newman (later Cardinal Newman), and the concept of 'muscular Christianity' in the writings of Charles Kingsley and Thomas Hughes. As a resident academic, Douglas was also 'Moral Tutor' at one of the university halls of residence—in the all-male bastion of Hugh Stewart Hall, or HuStu as it was dubbed in the collegiate lingo. While Willoughby Hall, where I was a Moral Tutor, was run on fairly liberal lines, HuStu still clung to such time-hallowed traditions such as 'Ladies' Night', where on the first Monday evening of each month residents were allowed to invite a female guest for dinner in Hall. In the autumn term of 1976 Douglas asked me as his dinner guest, and I accepted.

The dinner had a formal dress code. I consulted with Marion, my old friend from F Floor days, who was an excellent seamstress. Between us we bought a length of black fabric printed with tiny pink rosebuds and ran up a long skirt. Marion also ingeniously managed to produce a nice pink blouse with tiny puff sleeves from a remnant of *broderie anglaise*. On the appointed evening I fixed a tortoiseshell hair slide in my long brown hair and stood in front of the full-length mirror sucking in my stomach to try to achieve an hourglass figure.

'It looks OK—you'll do,' Marion said, eyeing me critically with sewing pins still between her teeth, 'but for God's sake, let your stomach out!'

Douglas first showed me the extensive collection of books in his rooms. There was a parlour harmonium in one corner at which he sat and started to play, working the pedals nimbly with his feet and pulling out the organ's stops while singing a hymn in the deep sonorous baritone that only Welsh male voices can produce. When the dinner gong sounded he escorted me into the Senior Common Room where various tutors, dons, Hall worthies and their guests had assembled. The long refectory table on a raised dais had been set with candles, crystal glasses, and silver cutlery. In the hall below sat the serried ranks of male undergraduates with their guests. We stood for the Latin grace: *Benedictus benedicat per Jesum Christum dominum nostrum ...*, after which everyone sat down and a great hubbub ensued. Sitting beside Douglas, I, along with everyone else around us, was hugely entertained by his non-stop banter and endless jokes. Food appeared before us on the table and we reached across to help ourselves from the dishes. It was then that I saw him. Diagonally across the table from me sat a mesmerizingly handsome man—a real Adonis.

My heart missed a beat as I surveyed his noble features—the soft wavy lock of brown hair on his brow, the kindly, twinkling eyes, and the fine lines at the corner of his mouth which crinkled so engagingly whenever he smiled. There was no mistaking the unsettling magnetic attraction deep within my core. Oh, what would I not give to get to know this man!

After dinner, Douglas, ever the impeccable host, suggested going back to his rooms for coffee, and: '…I'd like you to meet some of my fellow inmates…' Several young men duly arrived, and polite conversation ensued, laced with nice coffee and port. Then my heart missed another beat—the Adonis was also among this crowd! This was James, a young medical graduate of St Andrews and Dundee Universities who was taking a year out of hospitals to study for the notoriously tough Primary Examination of the Surgical Fellowship. Appointed a temporary Lecturer in Anatomy at Nottingham, his work involved preparing cadavers for dissection by undergraduates, teaching anatomy to medical undergraduates as well as to trainee physiotherapists and radiographers in the School of Medicine. It was a 9-5 job which allowed evenings for revision and study. James came and sat down beside me on the sofa. I kept my eyes down, but couldn't help stealing a few sidelong glances. Then he turned to speak to me and his arm accidentally brushed against mine. I was thrilled.

Many years afterwards I asked him what were his first impressions of me—had he been equally smitten? 'No, not really,' came the laconic reply with an amused smile, 'I just saw a nice-looking girl with a tassel of shiny hair who didn't talk crap!'

⚜

James and I got together after that, and dear Douglas, who had played Cupid, receded into the background, though he would remain a true friend to us both. Our relationship was tentative at first. We were both innocents—I was a complete novice and James was nowhere near being a Lothario. I got the impression that he was shy with women. Neither of us had played the field and we weren't keen to rush things. We enjoyed each other's company immensely, but in a restrained manner, happy to allow it to progress slowly. For me it was the beginning of an intoxicating time. I was totally smitten, and at last understood the sentiments behind the great love poems which I had so long admired—Elizabeth Barrett Browning's *Sonnets from the Portuguese*, Shakespeare's love sonnets, and allusions to unassuaged desire, such as in Robert Herrick's well-known lines:

> Whenas in silks my Julia goes
> Then, then, methinks, how sweetly flows
> That liquefaction of her clothes.
>
> Next, when I cast mine eyes and see
> That brave vibration, each way free,
> *O, how that glittering taketh me!**

(Herrick, *Upon Julia's Clothes*, * italics mine)

We were well suited to each other in many ways, James and I. We were both fluent in French (he had previously attended an International School in Paris). Also, as James's mother was South African he was naturally sensitive to cultural nuances and inherently tolerant of foreignness. Like me he had a great love of literature, books, art, and music. 'I bet you marry a nurse one day,' I would tease.

'Not a hope!' he always countered. 'I'd hate to have to talk hospitals all the time!'

James had a beaten-up old car, and on weekends he would call at Willoughby Hall for me. It made me the envy of most of the girls who peeked from their windows to witness the Moral Tutor's New Man—none of their boyfriends had cars! We would drive off to places like Southwell Minster, or walk in the Peak District. We attended concerts in town, and witnessed the unforgettable performance of a baroque opera in period Georgian costume in a stately home deep in the countryside. We saw some good films too, but were always too shy to hold hands in a darkened cinema.

Meanwhile, every Sunday morning I still regularly attended Stuart Burgess's Methodist Church, and the coffee mornings at his home afterwards. I had also begun to attend Evensong at the local 'high' Anglican church on Sunday evenings, which I loved for its candlelit silence and sacred music. It reminded me of my secret childhood forays into the Catholic Eglise de Sainte Thérèse in Geneva. For the time being, Iran and the expected censure of my Muslim family seemed far away. My MethSoc friends assumed that I was virtually on the cusp of a conversion, but for now I was quite happy to remain perched on the religious fence. I was in love with both the Church and 'in love with love'. James and I did discuss religion at some length, and while James, who had been raised as a Methodist, respected my spiritual leanings, he didn't feel a personal need to attend church regularly. Equally, I respected his reservations—after all, I was the one who was the renegade. Neither of us pressured the other to change, though spiritual inclination was perhaps the single main difference between us.

━━━❦━━━

The weeks passed, and I continued to bask in the enjoyment of my new status as Someone Special. It actually gave me the impetus to study harder and better. People started to comment on how well I looked. Every morning I woke up feeling really happy, taller, and even slimmer! Meanwhile James was also working hard—out all day at the Medical School then studying well into the small hours. It was late autumn and, with the submission of my great opus looming in the summer, I was on 'final approach' and I would soon be heading south to the Bodleian to check references. I left at the beginning of February 1977 for two months at Oxford. We didn't see each other during all that time, but we exchanged many letters. On the 14th of that month the postman delivered a small envelope inside which was an anonymous Valentine consisting of long pink ribbon with four cardboard cut-out heart shapes strung along its length at various intervals. For James, a self-professed unromantic who disliked displays of excessive sentimentality and what he called *schmaltz,* this gesture was a Big Deal, and I still treasure it.

James, 1977

James's parents resided within striking distance of Oxford, so we had arranged our eventual reunion to coincide with my final weekend at the hostel in Oxford. James was going to drive down from Nottingham and take me to 'meet the parents'. This was a significant watershed, and not something James had done often— if ever. I remember being nervous about making a good impression. I got my long hair trimmed in Oxford, and went shopping for a decent dress and a bunch of flowers for his mum. I need not have worried. His parents were charming and genuinely interested in my background. They themselves had met in Palestine during the Second World War and were therefore familiar with Middle Eastern culture and mores. Besides which, being South African, James's mother knew more than most people what it was to be a foreigner in Britain. His father was a quiet and self-effacing retired banker who was unfailingly kind. I think I made a reasonable impression on them both, and I assume it helped that I wasn't an airhead.

Later that day, after a lovely meal *en famille,* James and I went out for an evening walk through the frosty Warwickshire countryside. We held hands in silence and stood for a long time looking up at the bright starry night sky. Neither of us spoke, but our hearts beat as one. It was a defining moment. I felt that life just couldn't get any better. How was it possible that this most wonderful person with good looks, brains, nice manners, inherent kindness—and a doctor to boot (Oh, how pleased Baba would be!) actually liked *me*? I wanted be with him for ever, to 'cleave unto him' and to bear his children. How lucky was I, in the words of dear old Ivy who summed it all up in a pithy nutshell: '*...and he's not been snapped up!*' With God, it seemed, anything was possible.

It was early summer and the time for my viva voce examination was drawing near. Soon, God willing, I would be defending a successful doctoral thesis, and shortly afterwards I would be returning to Iran. James was due to sit the first round of his Surgical Fellowship exams imminently too. He had already secured his next post, that of Senior House Officer at the City Hospital in Nottingham—a step up on the ladder known as 'the Surgical Rotation'. What would then happen to us? Our relationship had arrived at a natural impasse. It would no longer be possible to continue indefinitely this courtship, innocent and old-fashioned as it was.

In reality it was quite unfortunate that we had only had a few months together—we had met in November, and it was now May. Six months was just not long enough. I dreaded the arrival of summer when we would be forced to part. In my uncomplicated mind there was surely only one foregone conclusion: we would eventually be together come what may. We could work something out—it would be either here in England, or perhaps even in Iran. True love involved constancy. Didn't the Bard famously say:

> Let me not to the marriage of true minds
> Admit impediments. Love is not love
> Which alters when it alteration finds...
>
> O no; it is an ever-fixèd mark,
> That looks on tempests, and is never shaken...
>
> (Shakespeare, *Sonnet 116*)

But it was complicated. And there were obstacles. James had his training to complete (the path to consultant surgeon would entail at least another six years of grind). And I had the financial bond to repay—to say nothing of a family back in Iran who fully expected to get their daughter back. A decision had to be made soon, and it was James who made it.

He had kept quiet until I had submitted my thesis, but I did feel an almost imperceptible drawing away from the delightful intimacy that we had so recently enjoyed. Surely I was imagining it. Resolutely burying my head in the sand I concentrated my efforts on preparing for my viva and put all negative vibes down to associated nerves. But there was no denying it, something *had* changed—I knew it, even before James came out with it:

'It's just not going to work—there are too many negative logistics, and everything is against us—the timing, cultural expectations, finances, employment.... You've got to return to Iran for several years, while I've got to stay here and complete my training…it's not right to have an unresolved question hanging over our lives at such distances for an unspecified length of time—it would be unfair to us both…etc…etc…etc….'

There it was, out in the open—the axe that felled my hopes.

***

During the many ensuing angst-filled discussions, James reassured me that he would always treasure our friendship in spite of this sad conclusion, but he truly believed that our chosen career paths were diverging, and that the time we had been given to get to know each other was in reality too short for a life-altering commitment. I didn't agree, of course, and the decision was his. I tried my best not to plead, even as my heart was slowly breaking into a million pieces. James looked terribly upset, like Brutus delivering the death blow, and I knew he hated himself for having to do this.

Later, as we met for a final farewell, I gave him a small book of poems as a keepsake. He took it from me almost reverently and placed it in the left breast-pocket inside his jacket, saying: 'See, it is close to my heart.' I nodded dumbly, bravely trying to fix for ever in my memory his features and beloved smile. I felt almost like Juliet: 'Good night …! Parting is such sweet sorrow' (*Romeo and Juliet*, Act 2, Scene 2). One last clasp of his arms, and then he was gone. Gone!

I ran upstairs to the top floor of Willoughby Hall, where I knew F Floor had a small window overlooking the quadrangle entrance. I looked below and saw James leave the building. I waved frantically, but he didn't look up. He strode head down, purposefully up the winding path and turned the corner. Suddenly he was out of sight. He was truly gone.

I went my room and sat down on the bed. Outside I could hear undergraduates chattering as they gathered for supper in the dining hall. In the distance I could see a hockey team running about on the playing fields. How on earth was it possible that life could just carry on as though nothing had happened?

For a long time I sat there, staring silently in the distance. Then, as darkness fell, I lay my head on the bed, buried my face in the pillow, and wept.

Beauty in Holiness

Chapter 6

THE SECRET WORLD OF GOD

I sobbed for what seemed like hours. When I finally dried my eyes it still felt as though a heavy stone was pressing on my chest. It remained so for days. Sometimes when things were going well I appeared to have got over my broken heart, but then I would remember, and it would catch my throat once more. My MethSoc friends rallied round offering commiserations—most of them had been through this kind of thing before, and I felt that some were privately beginning to get exasperated at my limpet-like clinging to a lost cause. In the end my good friend Marion came to the rescue and suggested I visit her in Northern Ireland. This had been a long-standing invitation for several years but until now I had always turned it down because Baba and Mami were dead against my going into what they perceived to be a war zone. Middle Eastern media regularly hyped-up the violent sectarian troubles in Ireland, keen to show that Christianity was not the peace-loving religion it liked to portray itself. 'Do you see anyone else taking holidays in war-torn countries?' Mami would ask. 'Catholics and Protestants are at each other's throats, and the IRA are killing people with guns and bombs! Shame on them! Why don't they follow their Jesus and "turn the other cheek" like they're supposed to?' In deference to these views, and trying to be a good daughter at a distance, I had always turned down Marion's invitation. However, I now decided that since I no longer cared if I were to be blown up by a bomb, I would ignore their advice. I told Marion that I would come. It turned out to be one of the best weeks ever.

Marion's family owned a small dairy farm with a milking parlour and a herd of about twenty cows near the Antrim coast. I never witnessed any violence during my stay, though there were occasional reminders like the soldiers posted outside every shop to search one's bags, and the sound of distant bursts of sporadic gunfire at night. Marion has four sisters and a brother, David, who helped their father on the farm. Her parents had rarely been further afield than Belfast or Dublin and were intrigued by their guest who was a foreign townie. Warm-hearted country folk, they adopted me as a family member and put me to work straight away feeding chickens and collecting buckets of pig swill. David and his dad would crease up with laughter at my innocent questions such as: 'Why don't your cows have bells around their necks?' 'Oh my God! She thinks this is the Swiss Alps!' More gales of laughter.

One night I was awakened from a deep sleep by Marion shining a torch into my face. 'Come on, hurry up and get dressed! One of our cows is birthing, and Dad thinks you'd like to see it.' I squelched after her to the barn in my wellies from where we could hear loud shouts and mooing. Labour appeared to have become obstructed, and the poor cow was having a hard time of it, thrashing about with her unborn calf's two forelegs protruding from her backside. Marion's dad tied one end of a rope around the little hooves and secured the other end to a wooden post in the middle of the barn. He and David tried to calm the beast while at the same time dodging its thrashing hindquarters as the animal jerked wildly, pulling on the rope with nostrils flaring and eyes wide with fear. 'If she doesn't deliver soon we're gonna have to summon the vet,' said their father. Finally, after a great deal of pulling, pushing and loud mooing, a wet baby calf plopped unceremoniously onto the barn floor. I watched fascinated as it immediately got up onto wobbly legs. 'Ah, that's better! Well done my girl!' said Marion's dad, patting the cow while David put down clean straw for her calf. Turning to me grinning he said, 'You'll not forget that in a hurry now, will you?' He was right—I've not forgotten it!

After all that excitement life seemed dull on my return to Nottingham. It was July and my plane ticket back to Iran was booked for 1st September. I was returning with the coveted academic degree I had set out to secure exactly five years after I had left home, and a university lectureship awaited me. Life seemed good on the surface, but underneath it all I felt unsure of my identity. Who was I? I didn't feel Persian, I wasn't English, I wasn't Swiss, I certainly wasn't Muslim, I wasn't even a Christian. Nor was I any longer someone's girlfriend. Existential questions like 'Who am I?' and even 'Am I?' swirled around my mind.

With still at least a month to kill before I was due to return home, I took myself off to St Beuno's, the Jesuit sanctuary in North Wales where as a student I had spent so many peaceful weeks. Ostensibly this was to say goodbye to my kindly mentor Father Peter, but I also knew it was a place where one could have a completely uninterrupted time with God. I needed to have this conversation with God once and for all because I felt I was being 'hounded' and I wanted it to stop. It wasn't my fault that He had placed me within a Muslim family who already worshipped Him in the approved way. I had tried my best—wasn't He satisfied? Or was...

...my gloom, after all,
Shade of His hand, outstretched caressingly?

(Thompson, *The Hound of Heaven*, 1893)

It was dusk when I got off the bus in the small hamlet of Tremeirchion in the beautiful Vale of Clywd and walked to St Beuno's, set high on a hill looking across the Welsh valley to the mountains of Snowdonia and the sea. Father Peter was waiting in his wheelchair at the top of the stone staircase. As I stepped into the hallway, assailed by the familiar scent of beeswax and catching a glimpse of the Jesuit motto AMDG (*ad majorem Dei gloriam*) inscribed over the lintel, I felt as if I was coming home.

After supper I poured out my misgivings and self-doubts. Father Peter was a great listener, and he just sat back and listened to my ramblings. Then he made a quiet suggestion: 'Would it help to try the *Spiritual Exercises*?'

Written in the sixteenth century by St Ignatius of Loyola, the Spanish founder of the Society of Jesus, the *Spiritual Exercises* are a compilation of prayers and contemplative practices which help to deepen one's relationship with God and to clarify one's spiritual vision. Divided broadly into four thematic weeks the meditations are traditionally undertaken as a thirty-day silent retreat, but may be adapted to meet various needs in modern life. Their underlying outlook is obviously Catholic, but they can be undertaken by Christians of any denomination. Father Peter said he would adapt them fit in with my travel and other plans: 'God may surprise you,' he suggested with a smile.

~~~~~

So it was that in July 1977 I entered the grand silence of a Long Retreat. The improbable nature of this alliance didn't escape me — the crippled priest, the Muslim girl, and the *Exercises* — even a scriptwriter would have been hard-pressed to invent it!

Father Peter was appointed as my Spiritual Director for the retreat and we met for one hour every day to discuss my progress. Surrounded by the Jesuit community of priests and lay brothers who went about their daily business, my days ran broadly according a circadian rhythm. Morning prayers in the chapel were succeeded by a silent breakfast, after which there was a period of study, followed by Mass which I attended as a quasi-postulant, then a solitary walk before lunch. In the late afternoon came Benediction when the sanctified Host was displayed in a beautiful monstrance to the plainchant accompaniment *Tantum ergo Sacramentum*. After supper I met with Father Peter, and later *Nunc Dimitis* would follow in the chapel along with Night Prayers.

During this retreat I read a number of seminal works by Christian writers in St Beuno's well-stocked library. I was especially moved by *The Imitation of Christ*, the work of fourteenth century mystic Thomas à Kempis. Written as an earnest conversation between God and a man of simple faith, the relevance of this mediaeval work to the lives of ordinary Christians in modern times is well-merited. Completely different, but equally inspiring, were two autobiographies from the 1940s which I read from cover to cover. The first was *The Seven Storey Mountain* by Thomas Merton, an American Trappist monk who craved the silence of the Cistercian Order, searching for faith and peace in a world which both fascinated and appalled him. The second was *I Leap Over the Wall* by Monica Baldwin, an ex-nun from the Order of Augustinian Canonesses who gave up the consecrated life after twenty-eight years, realising she had made a huge mistake. Both these works showed me that meaningful lives are not always perfect lives, and that even a fumbling search for God never fails to delight Him.

Father Peter McIlhenny SJ, at St Beuno's

As a non-Catholic, let alone a non-Christian, I did not partake of Holy Communion (though I had been granted dispensation for this from the forward-thinking Methodists), but my love of the

Eucharistic liturgy which drew comfort from the Immanent Presence of Jesus was all-encompassing. However, it was a guilty love, for I could never completely shake off my dyed-in-the-wool Islamic indoctrination that viewed even the symbolic consumption of a 'broken body' and 'cup of blood' as profane. So although I attended Holy Communion, I invariably felt like a spectre at the feast, or like a naughty child stealing sweets.

What I loved most of all was to sit in St Beuno's chapel after Mass. Its candle-lit and incense-laden interior enveloped me in velvety stillness like a protective caul. The faintly flickering light of the Reserved Host, symbolic of God's supreme sacrifice, shone in the darkness like a personal beacon and comforted me much as it had done in my clandestine visits to the church of my childhood. I wallowed in the luxury of having time to think about God, which seemed rarely possible in my daily life so full of noisy distractions. Prayer here was easier, more serene, like a gentle breathing-out and a breathing-in. I would sit or kneel for an hour at a time, and we would eye each other, God and I, in total silence. Eventually I would feel His eyes boring through me like gimlets, and I would be almost on the verge of telling Him that I wanted a 'let-out clause', to be left to become the ordinary Muslim that He seemingly had intended me to be, but I never did—of course, I knew that He already knew it anyway.

⁓✦⁓

Aesthetics had always played an important part in my attraction to Christianity. At an early age, in direct contrast to the spartan and tidy puritanism of my Muslim home life, it had been the ornate beauty of Catholic churches and Latin devotions that had first caught my imagination, and much later it was the aesthetic appeal of Wesleyan hymns with their beautiful words and tunes which held me in particular thrall. Thus I was initially drawn to Christ not merely through the Word, not merely through hearing the Good News, but also by the appeal of the beauty of holiness. I created and nurtured within myself a private world, a sacred space, filled with this beauty—my Secret World of God.

This aesthetic experience was probably unusual. Religious conversion is more commonly the result of evangelical endeavours, for it is evangelists who are true fishers of men. In the conversion accounts of ex-Muslims it's rare to find a mention of such aesthetic attraction, though this may have been edited out by fundamentalist scholars. My secret world was also unusual in that it had its seedbed in Roman Catholicism—a denomination which had largely ignored my presence on its fringes, and did not appear to be particularly interested reeling me in!

My Christian experience gradually evolved into something multifaceted, drawn from differing ecumenical strands, created over a number of decades, and in several different countries. It therefore also became 'liminal', or incomplete. Whichever way you looked at it I felt I would always be a misfit—too Christian for Muslims, too Anglican for Methodists, too 'high' for evangelical Anglicans, too sacramental for fundamentalists, too Protestant for Catholics. If I were I ever to be baptized, was it remotely possible that I might ever be considered a 'normal' Christian?

Little by little over the ensuing days, Father Peter managed to peel away some of the psychological barriers I had erected between God and myself, much like an onion's skin can be peeled back layer by layer to reveal its inner heart. Who was the God of my secret world? For years I had tried to pigeonhole Him into a neat religious box—my secretive Christian one, or the upfront Islamic one. Being a generous God of perfect timing, He had never forced Himself on me. There were things about Him that I didn't know or understand, and worried massively about not knowing—but then was it my place to know everything? Sometimes I gabbled things that I thought He'd like to hear, but I knew He really wanted to hear the truth, and He already knew what was in my heart. Eventually I came to the realisation that my angst about religious identity was not as tough as my ability to deal with it, and that the Holy Spirit would always guide me.

My greatest desire was to be baptized, but I also realised that there were many obstacles in the way, not the least of which was the commandment: 'Honour thy father and thy mother.' I knew that Baba and Mami would not be happy, and I didn't want to get baptized behind their backs and have folk in Iran saying things like: '…Unfortunately that's what can happen when young people go abroad and copy *farangi* ways…. at least be glad that she's not wading into boys and alcohol as well!'

Baptism would be an irrevocable step, like marriage, and I didn't want the sacrament to be trivialised as the sowing of wild oats in one's student days. Another obstacle was my perception that there was no church in Iran to which I could comfortably belong. While religious minorities—especially those 'of the Book'—were respected and free to worship according to their respective traditions, conversion from Islam, even in quasi-liberal days of the Shah, was a different matter. Islam, like Judaism, is intrinsically a faith rooted in racial heritage and those roots are deeply intertwined. Just as a Jew would always be a Jew, it would be difficult to convince Muslim Iranians that converting to Christianity was neither a rejection of the noble tenets of Islam, nor a rejection of one's cultural heritage. I wasn't aware of the concept of 'Persian Christian' *per se* at the time. I had been brought up with the notion that Iranian Christians were either from Armenian or Assyro-Chaldean cultural backgrounds, each with their own distinct racial heritage and their own unique language. The Orthodox Rite of Christianity to which they belonged pre-dated Islam, and was then accepted as one of Iran's 'official' religions, as were also Judaism and Zoroastrianism. Conversion out of Islam into Christianity, on the other hand, would always be perceived as apostasy. I knew I was not ready for such a step.

~~~⬥~~~

I completed the *Spiritual Exercises* in late August, emerging with a calmer frame of mind. I cannot pretend that it was easy. I struggled with the daily 'Examen of Conscience' as well as with the many 'colloquies', and admit to skipping blithely through quite a lot of the material. During my final week at St Beuno's, having daily listened patiently to my misgivings on the question of a formal Christian allegiance, Father Peter simply asked quietly, 'Have you considered that perhaps it's *not* God's will that you should become a Christian?'

On hearing those words I suddenly felt oddly light. Of course detachment is necessary if we want to follow God's will, otherwise we might be tempted to view the answer to prayer as a reflection of our own personal desires. Once I had accepted that a formal allegiance to Christ could wait—perhaps indefinitely—it felt as though a great weight had been lifted from my shoulders. St Ignatius might say that I had received a 'Consolation'.

Like the labouring cow on Marion's farm, after a lot of pulling and pushing—and, yes, even 'mooing' on my part—something new had emerged: the acceptance that God didn't want me to tuck myself away in a spiritual prison; He had set me free. Kicking my burden symbolically into an untidy bundle at the foot of Christ's cross, I walked away knowing it was finally time to stop hiding behind the walls of my Secret World.

The God of Surprises had indeed surprised me.

Tehran, 5th May 1978: the day of my baptism,
(Bishop Hassan Dehqani-Tafti is on my left and Rev Stephen Arpee on
my right)

PERFECT JOY

Tehran in the summer of 1977 was a city of two halves—on the surface smooth like a millpond, but dark with unknown debris beneath. Already as far back as 1975 in Nottingham my suspicions that politically all was not well back home had been raised by a letter from Baba stating that the two-party political system which at least had paid lip-service to democracy had been abolished by the Shah. From now on there would only be a single political party called the *Rastakheez* ('resurrection','resurgence'). All loyal citizens were required to join it.

Students in foreign countries like me were expected to register their loyalty to the new system by signing the relevant form at the Embassy of Iran in those countries. Baba demanded that I do so in London without delay. He, along with many of his generation whose education had been heavily subsidised by royal grants, was afraid that non-action might be interpreted as being an 'opposer of the regime'. I don't think he realised what a logistical burden that demand placed on me. Nottingham was nowhere near the heart of London where the Iranian Embassy was situated. With the Consulate's mornings-only office hours it would mean my having to find accommodation to stay overnight somewhere in the city simply in order to put my scribble to a piece of paper which I was certain would be summarily dispatched to a drawer. So I ignored Baba's injunction which he followed up over the next few weeks by several more written reminders. The whole futile exercise served to raise concerns that the country was entering an era in which the Shah was no longer held in complete reverence by his subjects.

When I returned to Tehran in September 1977 it was obvious that there were tensions in the air. Criticism of the regime, however innocent, could be sufficient grounds for imprisonment. But it was also no longer possible to stay out of trouble merely by re-fraining from open criticism. SAVAK began to round up writers, poets and intellectuals who failed to acclaim the current regime sufficiently, and it was rumoured that these people were punished for being 'Marxists'. Dozens of prominent clerics were also ban-ished from the country. Many people now appeared to have an acquaintance who had mysteriously disappeared.

On the surface life appeared stable in the Tehran of my family circle. Baba was still employed as an honorary lecturer in Public Health at the National University of Iran in Evin. This was also where I held a lectureship in the same English department where I had once been an undergraduate. We didn't talk about politics at home, and *Amu-jan's* involvement with SAVAK activities was never mentioned.

During that first year after my return home inflation rose dra-matically, and the government began to cut back on public ex-penditure which left many building projects unfinished. Hastily constructed dams failed to deliver water or electricity adequately in many areas, manufacturing profits fell, transportation facilities were inadequate to process the mounting deliveries of consumer goods waiting at the dockside in the Persian Gulf, and the price of basic goods rose even further. One of the most tragic failures of the Shah's innovative and laudable land reforms was that the plots distributed were often too small to yield a living, so peasants who had been dependent for centuries on feudal landlords were left with neither the means nor the expertise to succeed as modern farmers.

Migration to the cities to seek work soon became a flood, and those who found jobs in affluent north Tehran saw a very differ-ent kind of life—a city of Western decadence where supposedly observant Muslims frequented cafés and cinemas dressed in re-vealing clothing, and drank alcohol in *farangi*-style restaurants. Meanwhile, it was rumoured that the millions of dollars gleaned from the oil boom were being spent on military weapons. Further fuelling the disappointment felt by ordinary workers on low wages was the preponderance of white-collar foreign workers, especially Americans, on prodigious untaxed salaries. Resentment grew, and with it corruption and injustice. Simple working class people didn't understand all the fancy talk by government ministers. They had always sought for answers to problems from their local mullah who had prayed that God's will be done. But now vocal mullahs were being sidelined by politicians, and many villages were turning into ghost towns. Like most ordinary citizens our family's sole source of information was what we read in the press or heard on the local radio, but even I was now aware that this was not the same country I had left five years earlier—a feeling that was not merely the result of having grown a little older and wiser; there was definitely a faint menace in the air.

⚜

Against this backdrop I was welcomed home as an intellectual heroine, with friends and relatives coming round to congratulate Baba and Mami on my return: 'Hasn't she done well? You must be so proud—she's definitely the brainy one!' Some more well-meaning folk added: 'Make sure she makes a good match; she mustn't be allowed to become a *torshideh* ('soured') old maid—she needs a husband!' Baba and Mami knew my hopes of a permanent relationship with the shadowy James had been dashed. While they were outwardly sympathetic, especially as James was a doctor and would therefore have been a suitable prospective son-in-law, they said they had known it would never work—we were poles apart in all the requisites of a lasting union—family background, nationality, culture, religion. 'Love' apparently was ephemeral and wasn't a requisite of the equation. Their advice was: 'Forget him—there are plenty more fish in the sea!'

I began teaching at the Faculty of Arts in October of that year. My departmental colleagues were mostly young Iranians who had been educated abroad, but there were also a few British and American lecturers who were mainly the foreign wives of Iranians. We were an eclectic group but we got along fine. My students' English language skills were not really up to the mark; they struggled massively with the literary topics that were my particular remit. They were essentially students of English as a *second* language, not students of English literature. We had to go back to basics, and I ended up devising extra mini-courses in subjects such as Greek Mythology in order that they might try to understand Shakespeare and Milton.

One major problem was the lack of suitably simple reference material in the departmental library, and my students were not, on the whole, readers—they liked to be spoon-fed the basics and then to regurgitate the memorised information in their essays and examination papers. They demanded that lecture notes be typed up and distributed to individual students in the form of stapled 'polycopies'. By the time some of my colleagues retired they had actually written the equivalent of three or four textbooks-worth of 'polycopied' course notes! All this was a far cry from my own experience in England. Interestingly, most of the students actually believed they were really very good—after all they had excelled over hundreds of other hopefuls in the annual university *konkur* (from the French *concours* i.e. competition) in order to have gained an undergraduate place—and as far as they were concerned they were the elite. I sometimes wondered wryly what they would have made of the comment the Nottingham Professor of English had made to me: 'Go away, read for a few months, then come back and see me!'

Apart from the pedestrian grind of having to prepare and polycopy diluted teaching material, my university days weren't too full and I was able to also take on an extra job teaching English literature a few hours per week to secondary school students at an international school, the Parthian School, in nearby Evin. My pupils there were teenagers mostly of mixed parentage with an Iranian father and an English mother. My job was to prepare them for 'O Level' English (the British Ordinary Level of the General Certificate of Education). They were a great bunch of kids and it was nice to teach a small class of just five pupils as opposed to lecturing in a large amphitheatre full of undergraduates. At the end of the school year the English GCE 'O Level' examination papers were delivered to the school by diplomatic pouch via the British Embassy and the completed scripts returned in the same manner.

⚜

I still lived at home with Baba and Mami, but I was getting itchy feet. My sister Lilli was now married with a baby daughter, Maryam. She and her husband Hossein, a fellow social worker, had departed for the USA where they were both enrolled in post-graduate study programmes at the University of West Virginia. I didn't know it then, but from that point on Lilli and I would not see each other again for over thirty years, and we would become virtual strangers.

My parents had their own circle of friends with whom they socialised, often meeting for afternoon tea and playing endless rubbers of Bridge—a new craze among the older generation of middle-class Persians. At home they entertained with a regular *dowreh* ('circle' i.e. meeting of friends) on most afternoons, at which I was expected to be present as the polite and helpful daughter of the house proffering trays of tea and fruit. The regularity of this duty was starting to grate on me, and after five years of living independently I was ready to have my own space.

In the late 'seventies it was not unheard of for young professional women in Tehran to be sharing an apartment together. One of my Parthian School English colleagues, Sue, was looking for two flatmates to share a three-bedroom furnished apartment not far from us in the Yusefabad area. Another English girl, Ann, a marine biologist working for the Iranian fisheries industry, would be the third person to join us. Baba and Mami were not entirely happy with the idea of their unmarried daughter no longer living with them at home but in another house a few streets away.

'Whatever will people say?' Mami kept repeating. 'They'll think we must have had a bad argument...' However, because I was beginning to get on their nerves at home Baba eventually inspected the premises and agreed that the landlord and his wife who lived in the apartment below were respectable people and that the rent was not exorbitant. In any case I was now earning a decent salary. In the end it was agreed that I could go and live in the flat with the two English girls with the stipulation that under no circumstances were any lone men to be anywhere in the vicinity of our flat after 10pm. I finally got some measure of independence at the age of twenty-eight when I moved away from my parents and into the new apartment with Ann and Sue. We all got along fine. Each of us went out to work every day, returning home to cook and eat in the evenings. Ann and I became particularly good friends, and crucially it was Ann, a committed Christian, who first introduced me to the Persian Church which I hadn't known even existed. Curious to know where she worshipped, I asked her which church she frequented. 'St Paul's—the Persian Church, of course! There's a service every Friday in the English School.'

The English school of Tehran, officially named the Henry Martyn School after the eighteenth-century missionary and translator of the Psalms and New Testament into Persian, served as the premises of the Persian Anglican Church. It had a small indigenous congregation of Persian-speaking Iranians, mainly converts from Islam, but also from Judaism and Zoroastrianism, and in addition, a much larger congregation of English-speaking expatriates. The Episcopal Church In Jerusalem and the Middle East, to which it properly belongs, is a branch of the Anglican Communion which had been established following Church Missionary Society endeavours in the previous century. The Diocese of Iran is one of its four large dioceses, the other three being the Diocese of Egypt and North Africa, the Diocese of Cyprus and the Gulf, and the Diocese of Jerusalem (together with Lebanon, Syria, Jordan, Palestinian territories and Israel). At St Paul's Church in Tehran religious services were conducted in both Persian and English. Bishop Hassan Dehqani-Tafti, himself a convert from Islam, strongly upheld the view that the church's inherent Persian roots and culture were always its strength and he was keen that the church should maintain its Iranian essence. The accent was firmly on 'Christianisation' and not on 'westernisation'.

Because the early missionaries were keen to show the love of Jesus in action in Persia, they had established a large network of charitable organisations in the form of Christian hospitals and schools for the blind in cities like Isfahan, Shiraz, Yazd and Kerman. These institutions employed a large number of foreign Anglican and Presbyterian missionaries to keep them running. The danger of this hive of activity, especially for Muslim converts in the post-Revolution era, was that in becoming Christians and frequenting the company of such people, hard-line extremists might assume that they were aligning themselves to Western interests. This scenario, however, was yet to occur.

Friday is the Sabbath day in Islam and the one day in the week when people don't need to work. Innovatively, this church had switched its Sunday services to Fridays to make attendance possible for the majority. One Friday morning I accompanied Ann to the Henry Martyn School. St Paul's Church in Tehran seemed to offer everything I had hoped for in all my years of sitting on the religious fence, and I may never have come across it had it not been for branching out to live on my own away from my parents.

The priest in charge of the larger English-speaking congregation of mainly foreign expatriate workers and diplomatic staff was a young American pastor, the Reverend Stephen Arpee. His Iranian counterpart, the Reverend Khalil Razmara, who like Bishop Hassan was also a convert from Islam, was in charge of the much smaller Persian-speaking congregation consisting of first- and second-generation converts. Every Friday there were two church services at St Paul's, both of which included Holy Communion—one in English in the morning and another in Persian in the afternoon. In theory one could attend Divine

Service in both languages on the same day. The Persian congregation also met for Evensong on Friday evenings. I began to attend both services fairly regularly and felt instantly at home. At last I had found my church, a place of worship where I felt comfortable among folk from the same background as myself.

Rev. Khalil Razmara, St Paul's Church, Tehran

My eventual 'Road to Damascus Moment' was not preceded by a trumpet flourish or a flash of lightning, but it happened in a quiet moment one evening while I was at my desk writing. Suddenly I *knew*. I can't remember why I thought I *knew*—I just did. It was really that simple. After all those years of questioning, searching, deliberating, all the agonising over the pros and cons of conversion, none of it seemed to matter any more. I knew I had been a Christian at heart for a long time, but now I felt it was time to stop hiding and to declare it. I wanted to be purged of my past life, and to receive the sacrament of baptism. At the time I said nothing to Baba and Mami, but only confided to the two priests, Reverend

Stephen Arpee and Reverend Khalil Razmara. Both were quietly pleased, and Stephen said that he would prepare me for baptism for which I would require a course of instruction. Khalil was more cautious, and said it was really important that I should first meet our Bishop, Hassan Dehqani-Tafti, who lived in Isfahan, several hundred miles south of Tehran. It so happened that Bishop Hassan was due to visit Tehran soon, and a meeting was duly arranged.

I have never forgotten that meeting. It was to change my life. Bishop Hassan was a truly loveable man, and a real shepherd to his scattered flock. In time he became a surrogate father to me, as he also was to many others from all walks of life. We talked privately for a long time, and he impressed upon me that the road to baptism in Iran was fraught with practical problems. 'I would rather baptize a whole village than a single person,' he said, 'not because the numbers are greater, but because people who are in the same boat support one another when times are hard. A single person converting from Islam will be very alone in their faith.' His warning to me was that baptism could isolate me from my family and other Muslim Iranians. A convert would be in it for the long haul and would need the metaphorical stamina of a marathon runner in order to survive.

Then Bishop Hassan asked me a surprising question: 'Do you want to get married?' When I said yes, provided that the right man came along, he continued, 'Then I presume that in adopting Christianity you would want a Christian marriage?' 'Of course,' I replied. 'It goes without saying.' 'Well,' he said, 'I have to tell you that I have travelled all over this country as Bishop, and I have met all our congregations up and down Iran, and I can tell you now categorically that there isn't a pool of single Iranian Christian men your age or older! There is a blind Christian gentleman in Isfahan, and a divorced Christian fellow in Kerman, neither of whom presently has any desire to get married. If you are serious about becoming a Christian and having a Christian home in Iran, then by becoming a Christian in this country you may be closing the door on marriage and children. I want you to think about that carefully. Of course, there's nothing wrong in choosing to live a single Christian life. I have a number of women in my Isfahan church, notably a very nice Persian lady, *Sara-Khânum*, who like yourself converted to Christianity—and thereafter all offers of marriage dried up for her. She does many good works and is a pillar of our small St Luke's Church in Isfahan, but I know that she deeply regrets her spinster state. Be aware that this is a fate that could await you also if you proceed.' Sobering words, indeed!

I don't think any of my British and American Christian friends or acquaintances would have understood such over-arching potential implications of religious conversion. In the West conversion is simply a matter of personal faith, whereas in the East it is necessarily deeply rooted in the perception of one's culture, racial ties, and heritage, and it strikes at the very core of one's social identity.

I did go away and think about it, and I decided that the risk was worth the prize. Maybe it was just as well that James and I had parted company—now that marriage with the only person I loved was no longer on the cards, I could wholeheartedly and freely embrace a new life in Christ—it had finally become possible. Was I in danger of sublimating my hope of a physical love for the certainty of a spiritual one? Viewing it from the distance of several decades later I admit that perhaps there was a trace of sublimation present. However, I also believe that God works with what He already knows is present within our hearts.

Many people in St Paul's two distinct congregations in Tehran rejoiced at my final decision. Funnily enough, I made my momentous decision far away from all the Christian influences that had brought me to its brink. The Catholic parish of Sainte Thérèse in Geneva was oblivious about its early influence on my childish self, Methodist friends in Nottingham had moved on with their own lives, probably remembering me only as an earnest enquirer of Christianity, the Passionist Sisters in Leeds and Jesuit priests in

Wales went about their daily chores unaware that I had seen Christ's love shining through them all and that it had ultimately brought me to His feet. It hadn't happened quite how I had imagined it would, but once I had made my decision I never wavered—I knew it was completely right.

⚜

Telling Baba and Mami was no picnic, but for some reason it didn't turn out as the awful session I had imaged it might be. My parents had other things to worry about. Baba's health wasn't as robust as previously, there were clouds on the horizon of Lilli's marriage, *Khânum Bozorg*'s demeanour had become difficult as she began to get more senile, and there were rumblings in the foreign press about the activities of SAVAK which pointed a finger at *Amu-jan*. When, now adding to their worries, I told them that I wanted to be baptized in the Persian Church, Baba said he knew that I had become a Christian at heart a long time ago, but he questioned why I felt the need to take this public step which would jeopardise my social status and drag us as a family into a web of never-ending religious arguments. I managed to stand my ground and said that it was something that I felt was absolutely key to my future happiness and moreover that it would help me become a better person—but I knew that I was driving a dagger into their hearts. I promised them that I would 'do it' quietly, and that if anyone asked me outright I would tell them, but that everybody else who didn't know didn't have to know. Reluctantly, and somewhat unhappily, they eventually agreed—they said they wouldn't disown me, but begged me not to publicise it or tell the authorities. As far as they were concerned, I would officially remain a Muslim.

Actually, I was very fortunate that my decision was made during the Shah's reign when religion was still a reasonably liberal issue. God's timing was perfect. Had I waited just a year later when the country had become a militant Islamic state and everyone's concept of what being a Muslim meant radically changed, I may have decided not to get baptized because of the burden of

~ 141 ~

political implications for my family. I did secretly envy the second-generation Christians in our Persian congregation at St Paul's because if they were questioned by authorities they could always truthfully say that they happened to have 'inherited' their Christian religion from their parents who had converted before they had been born. This was a brilliant let-out clause to which I obviously had no recourse.

The disguised exterior of St Paul's Church, Tehran,
during the Revolution

One of the nicest Persian Christians of my own age whom I met in Tehran was Bahram, the son of Bishop Hassan. He was currently living in the same house as Rev Khalil Razmara and his wife in Tehran and he occasionally played the organ or piano for our church services at St Paul's. He had a great sense of humour and worked as a journalist for the Iranian media as well as having a locum teaching post in English a nearby college. Bahram had studied both at Oxford and at George Washington University and was extremely bright and articulate. He had a great future ahead of him.

During my period of instruction with Reverend Stephen in

Tehran, Bishop Hassan had invited me to visit him and the rest of his family in Isfahan. During the holidays I flew down to Isfahan and stayed with them in their home. He and his wife also had three daughters. Shirin, the eldest, and I hit it off straight away and we have remained close friends ever since. Bishop Hassan and his wife Margaret were wonderful people, and they became surrogate parents for all the converts in Iran, enriching the spiritual corners of their lives that their own families were unable to fill. There was no doubt in everyone's minds that their only son Bahram was destined for a very bright future. Bahram and I had some interesting conversations about God and the state of the country during coffee after the Friday services at St Paul's, and he became one of my favourite new friends in Tehran, most of whom were in some way connected to the Persian Church. None of us knew it then but Bahram would be dead within two years — murdered by Islamic extremists in the terrible aftermath of the Revolution. No reason would ever be given for this heinous act, but the bullet that killed him was probably intended for his father, Bishop Hassan. Bahram's death remains a source of infinite sadness to all who knew him.

✦

The day of my baptism, 5th May 1978, dawned bright and sunny in Tehran. Bishop Hassan travelled to Tehran from Isfahan to administer the baptismal rite and also to confirm me into the Episcopal Church straight afterwards. Baba and Mami knew it was an important milestone for me, and while they weren't at all enamoured by what I was doing, I overheard them saying that they were just glad that it was religion that I was addicted to — and not something worse.

I wore a simple summer dress, and I was supremely happy as I made my way through Tehran traffic to the Henry Martyn School. Because a large congregation was expected, the service was to take place in the sports hall of the school. In the past whenever I had anticipated this occasion I had always seen it my mind's eye as taking place in a traditional church setting complete with candles, organ music and stained glass windows—I had never imagined a venue which was really a glorified indoor basketball court with ceiling strips of neon lighting and posters about healthy eating pinned all over its walls. A wooden trestle table had been set up as a makeshift altar and stationed between the basketball goalposts at either end of the hall, over which were draped the heavy church altar cloths embroidered with the beautiful Persian Cross. Bahram was already seated at the school piano ready to play the hymns, and when he saw me he joked, 'Oh dear, here comes a not-so-innocent sheep!'

The hall was packed to overflowing that Friday. Much of the sacrament of baptism washed over me literally in a blur. Both priests in charge of St Paul's in Tehran, Stephen Arpee and Khalil Razmara, flanked Bishop Hassan as the prayers were read and he poured water over my head: 'You have now been clothed with Christ. May God who has received you by baptism into His Church, pour upon you the riches of His grace that within the company of Christ's people you may daily be renewed by His anointing Spirit and come to the inheritance of the saints in glory.' Bishop Hassan then proceeded to confirm me as a member of the Episcopal Church with the chrism by dipping his finger in the holy oil and making a sign of the cross on my forehead with the words: 'Strengthen, O Lord, your servant Farifteh with your Holy Spirit, empower her for your service and sustain her all the days of her life. Amen.'

After that, I was raised to my feet by both priests and presented to the congregation to general rejoicing and applause. Following this came the sacrament of Holy Communion, which the three priests concelebrated and of which I officially partook for the very first time. At last I felt I had Come Home.

Back home at the flat Ann and I had a celebratory lunch, and then we just got on with the rest of our day. Outwardly nothing had changed, but deep within my heart there was now abundant peace. Perfect joy.

Ayatollah Khomeini returns to Iran, February 1979

CHAOS

The first inkling that something wasn't quite right in Iran was in August 1978 when it was reported that four hundred innocent people had burned to death, trapped behind the locked doors of a cinema in the southern city of Abadan. Most people blamed this dreadful act on SAVAK, though later investigations indicated that a group of radical Islamic hardliners had actually been responsible. The Rex Cinema disaster was only the beginning.

Demonstrations incited by strikes and political protests began to take place in many towns. My flatmate, Sue, didn't return to Tehran after her summer break in the UK. She wrote to say that the British Embassy had advised caution against British nationals travelling to Iran. Ann and I continued to live in the flat for a while and carried on with our respective jobs. However, the mood at my university was turning ugly. Students were skipping lectures, congregating in animated huddles and wasting valuable class-time by posing questions loaded with political innuendoes. At the Parthian School my classes carried on as normal, but since this school was situated near to the infamous Evin Prison, access to its entrance was often blocked by Jeeps, police vehicles and soldiers. Just before Christmas Ann went home on leave, and although she tried valiantly to return in January she was unable to find a flight from London back to Tehran. I spent a few weeks on my own, then cut my losses and returned home to live with Baba and Mami. In the ensuing months political unrest escalated and any dreams my parents may have had about a peaceful retirement rapidly faded.

Still basking in the warm afterglow of my recent baptism helped me to overcome the suppressed panic that afflicted many others during this unsettling time, and mercifully enabled me to view the enfolding events in a slightly more positive light. St Paul's Church in Tehran didn't stop its Friday services, but as the weeks went by the number of expatriate worshippers declined dramatically. Universities and colleges eventually closed indefinitely in a bid to disperse the mounting student demonstrations. Sitting at home all day with nothing to do was becoming a regular occurrence. When I heard that a small number of British Embassy and British Council staff who attended St Paul's Church, among them Johnny Graham the British Ambassador to Iran (later Sir John Graham, OBE), were urgently seeking a teacher to help them with conversational Persian, I applied for and was appointed to the post. I started private tutoring in *Farsi* at expatriates' homes in Tehran. One thing led to another, and before I knew it I had also secured a part-time job at the British Embassy as a radio translator of Iranian News. These *ad hoc* jobs filled a void and provided me with some welcome academic and social contact.

Getting to the British Embassy from our house was unpleasant. Tehran's roads were now permanently choked with armoured tanks, Kalashnikov-toting soldiers, and cars blasting their horns as if Armageddon was at hand. The British Embassy was situated on Churchill Avenue in the older part of Tehran near the main Bazaar where political demonstrations often originated. In its heyday Churchill Avenue had been a pleasant, leafy boulevard bordered by mature lime and plane trees. Baba remembered the Tehran Conference of the Big Three allies—Churchill, Stalin, and Roosevelt—taking place there at the British Embassy during World War II in 1943. Now the high walls surrounding this magnificent building were regularly daubed with unsightly anti-British graffiti. (Post-Revolution this regal road would be renamed 'Bobby Sands Avenue' in memory of a notorious IRA hunger striker.)

After gaining entrance to the Embassy gate and having been dutifully searched by the guard, one stepped into a completely different world, a lovely 'Little England' with ornamental fountains and whitewashed porticoed bungalows which served as offices set amid pleasant gardens. Posters with incongruous rubrics such as 'BUY TICKETS NOW FOR YEOVIL REGATTA!' were attached haphazardly to the wrought-iron lampposts. I was allocated a desk in the Newsroom and presented with a set of headphones. My remit was to listen to the lunchtime news which was broadcast in Persian on Radio Iran, to translate it into English, type up three copies of my translation, and deliver them individually to the mailboxes of the British Military, Air and Naval Attachés. In the pre-Internet era this was the only way non-speakers of Persian could discover what Iranian media was saying daily about the escalating political situation in the country.

I now realise that it was foolish of me to have accepted such a position. Had I been found out, the political implications for my family would have been far reaching. But at the time we ordinary citizens didn't see a revolution coming, and neither did anyone suspect the demise of a monarchy which had existed for thousands of years. Fortunately I was considered to be an unimportant temporary employee and was largely ignored by the authorities. Needless to say, that job didn't last very long—the British Embassy was eventually forced to close, and diplomatic ties between our countries eventually ceased altogether. Johnny Graham left his post as Ambassador and returned to the UK. He and I have remained friends, and we still exchange letters. Although now fairly elderly, his mind is as sharp as ever, and his fondness for Iran remains undimmed. One of his recent letters to me contained the following heartfelt message: 'Ah, Iran, how my heart bleeds for her!'

Driven into a corner by insurgence, the Shah finally ran out of patience, banned all demonstrations, and imposed martial law. On 8th September ('Black Friday') a huge demonstration took place in downtown Tehran. Barricades were set up in the working-class area of Jaleh Square and military troops were deployed to instil order in the crowd. The demonstrators refused to move and the soldiers opened fire. Many innocent people were gunned down. One of my cousins was a doctor on duty at the hospital that day and she reported that dozens of mangled bodies had been brought in on stretchers, many bleeding to death in the corridors owing to the lack of medical staff and supplies. Some of the young bodies were those of the *Gard-e-Javidan*, the Shah's 'Immortal Guards' who had evidently deserted. The country descended into chaos.

The imposition of martial law and a curfew affected everyone. In practical terms it meant that you weren't allowed on the streets after 8pm. This might seem reasonably late according to Western standards, but in the Middle East most shops do their best business at sundown after the heat of the day has passed, and the timing of the curfew was early and disruptive. It basically curtailed any socialising—you couldn't visit anybody after work because you would have to be back home before 8pm. If anyone was caught out that person would have to spend the night there or risk dodging the street soldiers on patrol.

Municipal utilities such as electricity and water were cut off during the curfew hours. Everyone had to collect and store water during the day in order to have it available in the evening for washing and drinking. In some areas of Tehran a rumour went round that the capital city's water reservoir had been poisoned, ramping up the fear. Woe betide anyone with an electric cooker— when the electricity was cut off the stove was also defunct. You could only cook a meal if you had a gas appliance. Our stove used bottled gas, and the bottles soon ran out and there were no more deliveries, so eventually we ate everything cold and stopped cooking altogether. Darkness reigned everywhere at nightfall. There were no street lights, and no lighting in the stairwells of apartment blocks. People got stuck when lifts jammed between floors, and shops soon ran out of candles and matches.

I am often asked how we coped psychologically during that uncertain time. I think it was probably worse for people of my parents' generation who remembered the World Wars. They could foresee the disintegration of social order, and sensed that they might not live to see it right itself. I don't remember being afraid of that. Since no one knew what was going to happen I didn't imagine that the worst might happen. People who have lived through the Blitz in Britain often speak of the camaraderie that prevailed in the underground shelters where complete strangers helped one another and class distinctions didn't exist, and this spirit of camaraderie also prevailed among our younger generation. As a newly-minted Christian I was able to accept events with the detachment that comes from a complete trust in God. As trite as it sounds I felt the Holy Spirit immanent, and Christ ever present. Faith was able to give me a detachment and sustain me as nothing else could have done, and helped me to remain fairly optimistic. While my parents predicted chaos and meltdown, I shrugged off such worries with the insouciance of youth.

During the months of martial law in Iran there was no TV, no cinema, no media, and ostensibly no parties or social meetings. In the morning we would run the taps and fill bowls, sinks and bath-tubs with water which we covered and saved for later. Then we hurried to the shops and bought whatever groceries were available. If you had a job you worked, then hurried to get home before sundown. If you thought you might miss the curfew then you took a toothbrush and a change of underwear with you, as you would have to stay wherever you had got stuck at 8pm. People made their own entertainment. This often meant that rather than becoming isolated you actually grew much closer to your neighbours, as a true spirit of friendship born of necessity developed between strangers.

Older friends of Baba and Mami often dropped by to drink endless glasses of tea and to discuss the latest politics. I occasionally went out to friends' houses for a meal, and I once had to spend the night in a sleeping bag on someone's floor, unable to get home before the curfew. A few others were also there and were similarly caught out that night. We all lay convivially in a semi-circle on mattresses in our hostess's darkened sitting room chatting far into the night by the light of a single candle flickering on a saucer set between us on the linoleum floor, half-ignoring the sporadic bursts of gunfire in a neighbouring street. The next morning we realised that there had been a shooting nearby and cars had been set on fire.

By November the grim political situation had escalated. There were increasing reports of round-ups. University students were now free to roam the streets and many did so, dressed in black and carrying placards with anti-Shah and anti-government slogans. The Parthian School finally closed its doors, and its foreign staff left the country.

From his French residence in Neauphle-le-Château, Ayatollah Ruhollah Khomeini, the charismatic mullah whom the Shah had exiled to Iraq and who had since fled to Paris, was fuelling dissatisfaction with the Iranian regime by blaming the Shah for the country's every ill and preaching against the Western decadence into which it had fallen. His sermons were regularly distributed clandestinely in the form of pirated cassette tapes which were broadcast via loudspeakers in mosques and coffee houses everywhere. Popular bitterness against the Shah rose to a fever pitch. In the end, any compromise appeared to be impossible and the escalating stalemate could only be resolved by the departure of the Shah. There was an implacable demand that he abdicate, and in December of that year he was forced out.

On the morning of 16th January 1979 there was a tremendous, cacophonous hooting of car horns and raucous shouting in the streets. We could see soldiers jumping up and down jubilantly and embracing one another. Turning on the radio we heard that the Shah had left the country with his Queen and a small entourage. Before boarding the aircraft he bent down and scooped up a fistful of dirt—'a handful of Iranian soil by which to remember my dear country,' he is said to have whispered. Ostensibly he had left for a holiday. What the nation didn't know then was that the Shah was already terminally ill with cancer.

After his departure martial law and the curfew were lifted and the streets of Tehran erupted into a macabre show of euphoria amid the chanting of *Shah raft! Shah raft!* ('the King has gone!') No one guessed that the monarchy was finished for ever. Two thousand and five hundred years of imperial rule, all our nation had ever known since almost the dawn of its civilization, was wiped out in that single ignominious moment.

For our family it was an awful time. Baba's great friend, the elder of the two Nassiri brothers, whom we always respectfully called *Aghayé Senator* (Mister Senator), had been arrested out of the blue and taken away to prison. He was older than Baba by a few years and then already well into his seventies. Baba was devastated. No one knew where he was or why he had been taken. The assumption was that he had been arrested and imprisoned because he had been a statesman in the Shah's government.

Anyone with the hint of an association to the Pahlavis was now at risk. An entire generation of workers who had been at the forefront of the Shah's modernisation programmes in Iran was now being hunted down by self-styled vigilantes keen to rid the country of any links to monarchy and imperial rule. The implication of Senator Nassiri's arrest was that the safety of his younger brother, *Amu-jan*, the army general in charge of SAVAK, now hung in the balance. Baba and the entire Nassiri clan were mutely anguished, not daring to ask about the whereabouts of *Aghayé Senator* in case other family members were also hunted down and similarly carted off.

But the axe next fell on Baba himself. The National University of Iran posted a list of staff members whom they considered had been allied to the Shah. A large notice was nailed to the doors of the Medical Faculty with Baba's name as its heading and beneath it in large letters, the rubric 'Refused Entry to This Establishment Due to Following Crimes'. There followed a numbered list of Baba's purported 'crimes' which included the award of Pahlavi Foundation grants enabling public sanitation measures—the installation in rural areas of clean water and sewage disposal, the drainage of swamps to prevent the spread of malaria, and leprosy eradication campaigns. On hearing about this, Bahram confided to me that Baba's purported 'List of Crimes' would serve as a successful CV in any humanitarian organisation in the Western world! Baba was declared *matrood* (an epithet we hadn't heard of much before, variously meaning: 'despicable', 'outcast', 'expelled'), and the university barred him from re-entering its premises. He never set foot there again.

One morning I awoke early to the smell of burning coming from the kitchen, and when I ran down to investigate I saw Baba standing in his pyjamas before our gas stove systematically burning piles of photographs and papers. He had already destroyed various letters, certificates and papers by ripping them to shreds and feeding them to the flames. The charred remnants of a number of memorable photos taken of Baba with the Shah in Geneva, and others of him with the Shah at public health centres which he had helped to set up had been consigned the dustpan and the kitchen bin. Baba's entire professional life had been involved with public health measures in Iran, and these had obviously relied heavily on grants from the Royal Foundation. Fearful now that this would be viewed negatively by revolutionaries and lead to interrogation or worse, Baba was ridding himself of all potential evidence. It was tremendously sad to see this upright citizen's entire working life reduced to mere ashes on a domestic stove.

In the same week I caught Mami in the dead of night in the street outside our house emptying unopened bottles of alcohol down a municipal drain. During our years in *Farang* many visitors from Iran who had passed through the duty-free shop at the airport had given Baba and Mami such bottles as gifts. My parents were strictly teetotal, but they did offer drinks to their guests. When they moved back to Iran and we unpacked all our stuff, this stash came to light, having been carefully packed into boxes by the removal firm. Being a frugal person Mami hadn't thrown them out, but had stored the bottles of alcohol in a kitchen cupboard. Now the fear that our premises might be searched and we could be accused of disregarding an important Muslim tenet prompted her to dispose of their contents one at a time under cover of darkness into the city drains. What to do with the empties was another problem. It would be too risky to have a pile of empty whisky, gin and vodka bottles in the house. Mami and I wrapped them singly in newspaper, deposited them into our kitchen garbage and buried them deep under household waste. The whole operation, done by stealth, took us nearly a week.

While our lives were slowly being governed by fear, Baba and Mami were also living with a daughter who had supposedly betrayed them by rejecting their faith. In the Islamic theocracy that Iran had now become, my recent baptism posed a problem. Baba was afraid that authorities would discover he had fathered a daughter who had rejected Islam and who had been observed to hobnob with British and American infidels. I would be seen to be the fruit of a rotten tree which had to be chopped down. It added to the apprehension that as a family we would all somehow be punished.

One day when I went back to my desk in the university to collect some belongings, I was approached by a gang of students and rounded up, along with other departmental staff, and told that we were all going to be put on trial. We weren't frightened at that stage because these were students we knew quite well, and we assumed they were just showing lip-service to the principles of the new Revolution. We vowed to stand together and to accept no nonsense from any of them during any mock trial. We also agreed that if any student made an inappropriate or false allegation against any one of us that we would be united in defending our mates. That this didn't occur was soon to become abundantly clear. We were marched *en masse* into the largest lecture theatre and put through a so-called 'trial' by an illegal kangaroo court consisting of a jury of twelve of the very worst students in our faculty—worst, that is, in terms of grades, application to study, achievement, and general behaviour. They sat in a trumped-up jury box which they had constructed on an elevated dais along two rows of seats. One by one we were paraded in front of this 'jury' and made to answer for our 'crimes'. In my case this was principally the award of poor marks for poorly written English essays. I was later to understand that the content of these essays all contained a subtle political agenda which I had not understood and therefore ignored, awarding grades solely on the basis of English composition. Several older male colleagues who were able to answer back appropriately when accused, were duly exonerated by this joke-of-a-jury, and freed. As soon as they heard their 'not guilty' verdicts they simply slunk away, grateful to have been let off lightly. Not a single one of this group of colleagues made any attempt to stand behind the rest of us who weren't so fortunate— so much for their prior claims of solidarity!

By the time it was my turn I was shaking with apprehension. The charges were quite ludicrous but any attempt on my part to answer back was shouted down with guffaws and derisive comments from this jury who seemed only bent on destroying my character. In a short space of time I was declared guilty as charged, and escorted into a dark side room at the back of the lecture theatre to have my fingerprints recorded. A nervous first-year student was in charge of this task which he accomplished by dipping every single one of my fingers into a pool of ink and recording the results one by one on a paper with my name in bold letters. He also carefully recorded the digit and the hand from which each fingerprint was taken. The room was small and windowless, like a cupboard, and I was seized by panic when I realised that no one knew exactly where I was. If I were to disappear now no one would find out what had happened to me. It wasn't so much the fear of an unknown fate that I dreaded, as the inability to communicate with the outside world, and an incredibly deep and gut-wrenching regret that my disappearance or demise might leave no trace at all.

Fortunately for me, after this marathon fingerprinting session the student seemed unsure of his next move and he opened the door. While he was deliberating his next move I seized the opportunity to escape. I walked purposefully and as fast as I could towards the car park, jumped into my car and managed to get almost halfway home before I was stopped in the street by a gun-toting soldier who waved me to the side of the road and told me to get out. 'Excuse me *khânum*,' he said with uncharacteristic politeness, 'please get out, we need this car!' Thankful that I wasn't about to be arrested just yet, I handed over the car keys, grabbed my bag, and walked away. I never saw my car again, but I no longer cared. I managed to get home somehow, walking for miles at dusk through streets lined with tanks, demonstrators, and even looters. I finally arrived home hours later, trembling and incoherent. Mami put me to bed with a hot water bottle and a cup of tea. 'That's it,' she said. 'You're never ever going back!' And this time I agreed. Despite my lucky escape and the knowledge that Christ was always at my side, I had looked into the mouth of a nameless abyss, and I was scared.

In early January 1979 they came for *Amu-jan*. One day he was there and the next day he had simply vanished. Rumour had it that he had been arrested along with a number of other army generals and was going to be tried for crimes against democracy. His immediate relatives dispersed. Some of the Nassiris came to our house and we huddled together around our television set, wrapped in blankets against the freezing cold. We sat up all night waiting for any news. News only came days later, and it was terrible. A photo newsflash showed a handcuffed *Amu-jan* being hauled in front of the cameras, taunted by faceless interrogators. We watched horrified as he was shoved and harassed by a baying crowd. We could see that his face was bruised and that he had the scars of beatings around his head. Baba could bear no more and left the room. His family were in tears and wailing loudly. In the following days news bulletins kept portraying images of gallows from which dangled lifeless corpses. We were led to believe that *Amu-jan* had suffered a similar fate and denied a proper funeral. To this day none of my immediate family knows where his body is buried.

A few days later *Amu-jan's* older brother, the by now frail and elderly *Aghayé Senator*, was brought back from prison and deposited unceremoniously in the street outside his home. He was completely mute. Although his elderly wife and other relatives nursed him back to a semblance of health, he remained mute. Baba went to visit him daily, gently talking to him of their carefree boyhood in Semnan and reciting the verses of Persian poetry which they had both so loved. *Aghayé Senator* was either unable or unwilling to respond. He never spoke again. He hardly ate anything any more, and one day he just turned his face to the wall and died, never having uttered a single word. No one ever discovered what had happened to him during his incarceration, and not long afterwards his loyal and grief-stricken wife also died.

With the passing of these influential Nassiris, their remaining family dispersed—some went into hiding, others left Iran if they were able to, and by any means possible. We did not dare to enquire where they had gone. Baba's most influential Semnani friends were now dead or gone. He alone remained from that hopeful trio of boys who had grown up in Old Persia to become important in New Iran. The *rammâl* had predicted that one of the Nassiri brothers would become the 'Sultan's Comrade' and the other a 'Warrior', and this prediction had indeed come to pass, but both were now dead—Oh, how had the mighty fallen! Only the young lad destined to become a 'Healer' remained. Baba concluded that the reason he had been spared was because of the following fact: 'Doctors aren't important—they don't influence affairs of state.'

On the first day of February 1979, the exiled Ayatollah Khomeini's Air France jumbo jet landed at Tehran airport. It seemed as if the whole nation had pinned their hopes of a better life on this one individual. A French journalist asked him what his thoughts were about returning to Iran. He famously replied, *'Hichi'* ('nothing'). That freezing morning a million people lined the route of his motorcade, bringing the city to a virtual standstill. Thousands of villagers had walked for days like pilgrims in order to witness the

Ayatollah's return. Tehran erupted into a frenzy of euphoria. Bakers opened their shops and distributed free cakes, even tossing them directly at the crowds in the street. Tanks rolled down Tehran's boulevards with soldiers sitting on top of the gun carriages sporting stems of red carnations between their teeth or in the muzzle of their rifles.

While these macabre scenes were taking place ours wasn't the only family who stayed away, but we nevertheless stood at our windows cautiously waving to the passing processions in case our house was targeted as harbouring folk who were 'Anti'. Anti-what? We didn't exactly know, but we feared it nonetheless. It seemed that the nation had been united in getting rid of the Shah, but once the monarchy was overthrown everyone wanted something different to replace it. The goals of the Islamic Marxists clashed with those of the Marxist-Communists, Islamic Fundamentalists, Islamic Republicans, Hezbollahis, Baseejis, National Democratic Front, Muslim Republican Party, Fadayeens, Moderates, Mujahedins, Freedom Movement, etc. The nation became divided against itself. No one appeared to be in overall charge. Instead of abating, chaos continued to reign supreme. It was the state of affairs that William Butler Yeats had described so eloquently in his poem of 1919:

> Turning and turning in the widening gyre
> The falcon cannot hear the falconer;
> Things fall apart, the centre cannot hold;
> Mere anarchy is loosed upon the world,
> The blood-dimmed tide is loosed and everywhere
> The ceremony of innocence is drowned;
> The best lack all conviction, while the worst
> Are full of passionate intensity.

(Yeats, *The Second Coming*)

I would love to be able to say 'order was eventually restored', but what order appeared to have been restored was a mere semblance of real order. In the spring, cities limped back into gear, but the universities and colleges remained closed and faculty staff who were considered to be 'undesirable' were sacked by the new regime. It didn't really affect me as I had already been 'purged' from the system by becoming *matrood*. Sitting at home all day doing nothing except to mull over my fate was starting to jar on my nerves.

As time went on more and more friends and acquaintances just seemed to vanish. St Paul's Church services in Tehran which I had attended regularly in the last few months, and which I looked forward to immensely as a source of comfort and social interaction, now began to become more sporadic, and they stopped altogether after the horrific murder of our Persian priest in Shiraz, the Reverend Arastoo Sayyah. The Church Missionary Society in Britain and America withdrew their missionaries and our congregations grew smaller and smaller. Bishop Hassan was targeted and shot by revolutionaries at home in Isfahan while sleeping, but he survived the attack, as did his wife Margaret who needed hospital treatment. Our diocesan secretary, Jean Waddell, was also shot by extremists in Tehran and badly injured.

The small Persian Church went 'underground' in an attempt to draw less attention to itself. In Tehran we began to meet in one another's houses, but owing to traffic restrictions and communication problems (no mobile phones or Internet in those days) this was a far from satisfactory solution. Reverend Khalil Razmara administered Holy Communion when he could, but I think I received the Eucharist only once during all those months. Eventually the entire system broke down as any meetings were considered too dangerous, and our church services stopped altogether.

As a newly baptized Christian hearing the roar of those Hercules aircraft in the skies above Tehran taking away the many foreign Christian friends I had made, and on whose company I realised that I had relied quite heavily, was one of my loneliest-ever moments. It felt as though a carpet had been suddenly whipped from beneath my unsteady feet. The Persian Church had always been heavily dependent on the support—both material and spiritual—of foreign missionaries and committed Christians in various medical and teaching fields. They had been present in Iran from the earliest days of evangelism in the nineteenth century, and their untimely departure left a gaping void. As a fledgling church we were suddenly and frighteningly completely on our own. How would we be able to carry on without that sterling support? It was really a case of having to survive or be wiped out altogether. As in the parable of the mustard seed, we Persian Christians, 'the Faithful Remnant', were like a miniscule seed, presently buried and out of sight. If the soil in which we lay was fertile we had the potential in time to grow into a shade-giving tree. It was now all up to this tiny seed's potential—and against many odds my own life was somehow embedded within that seed.

⚜

Ignominiously freed from the shackles of teaching and lecturing. I now looked elsewhere for gainful employment. I didn't find a proper job, but I volunteered as a translator/interpreter at the Notre Dame de Fatima Hospital in Tehran which was situated near our home in Yusefabad. This hospital had been funded by a Catholic organisation to treat the poor, and was at the time staffed mainly by British doctors and Irish nurses who hadn't fled the country, but had not yet been in Iran long enough to master the Persian language. Their patients were needy, often illiterate, and spoke no English. Consequently the hospital recruited a team of volunteer translators to attend outpatient clinics and to interpret the dialogue between doctors and patients during the consultation. I was given a white coat to wear and sent all over the hospital to do these translations—I once even ended up in the labour ward to talk a young village girl through the birth process while doctors and midwives were busy exhorting her from the nether regions of the delivery couch! I loved this locum job and got on well with the Matron who had never married and had dedicated her entire life to nursing and training nurses in the mission field. I confided to her a bit about my background and current lack of prospects.

One day she asked me whether I might be willing to consider going to England to train as a nurse: 'Britain's crying out for nurses just now,' she said, 'and I know for a fact that my own hospital, St George's in London, is moving this summer from its magnificent historical spot near Marble Arch to new premises south of the Thames in Tooting, and is currently seeking several extra intakes of trainee nurses. You're fluent in English, you enjoy hospital routines, you're reasonably intelligent—I'm sure you'd make a good nurse! Besides you'll not get your lectureship back, and as a Christian convert you're a complete misfit here in Iran— *you've nothing to lose!'*

At first this seemed like a ludicrous suggestion. Why on earth would I train to become a nurse in my thirties when I had spent all my adult life studying a completely unrelated discipline— literature? I knew next to nothing of biology and had tried to steer clear of any allied subjects involving science or maths at school. It was a crazy idea. Nevertheless the more I mulled it over, the more attractive the proposal became. Baba and Mami were not over-enthused by the idea, but they were also acutely aware that my present situation was problematic. I know that there ensued between them a series of private discussions along the lines of 'We Need to Talk About Farifteh.' By now they realised I would not relinquish my Christian faith. In any case I was also *matrood*—an outcast, and unemployed. Also, they feared that in the present repressive climate, someone might eventually spill the beans on the disgrace of my apostasy from Islam.

Baba had a much younger stepsister living in London, my Aunt Mehri. She had married an English doctor in the 1960s, and they had three sons. They had been in the United States during all the time I had been in Nottingham so I hadn't met them in years, but they had recently returned to live in London where Mehri's husband was a cardiologist. It was conceivable that I could stay with them for a while and apply to St George's Hospital as a trainee nurse. I didn't know whether I was really cut out for nursing, but I did know that the idea of returning to England seemed attractive. I was fed up with life in post-revolution Tehran. Living with Baba and Mami was tolerable but I felt stifled by their endless *dowrehs* where people came to discuss politics and reminisce about life in old Iran and the awfulness of the present situation. I craved a job, independence, freedom.

Somehow it was mutually decided that I should give it a try. In any case, I wouldn't be allowed to leave the country scot-free or indefinitely—at the very least I would need a ticket with a firm return date stamped on it. As this plan slowly started to take shape, I even allowed myself to feel cautiously excited. I prayed about the decision but couldn't decide whether this was what God really wanted me to do. However, I have a rather impetuous nature, and, being someone who will often leap before taking a good look, I thought I would go anyway! What was there to lose? I could always come home—couldn't I?

Perhaps it was just as well that none of us knew then that some twenty years would elapse before I would return.

St George's Hospital, London, 1979
(I am in the middle row, 1ˢᵗ on the left)

RISING FROM THE ASHES

Getting out of Tehran six months after the Islamic Revolution was not easy. Self-styled student revolutionaries had taken politics into their own hands at my university, and because no one had been appointed in charge of academic affairs, they were still wielding control. Anyone intending to leave the country needed an exit permit issued by his or her employer. Even though my post had disappeared in the post-revolutionary purge of academic courses, as a university employee I still needed a permit sanctioned by the Chancellor to enable me to travel. Colleagues whose erstwhile studies abroad had similarly been funded by a grant from the Shah's government consulted lawyers over the situation regarding the conditions of our employment bond, and the general consensus was that because our contracts had been axed by the government we were now technically free of this bond. However, that particular 'government' had been hastily convened in the aftermath of the Revolution in a period known as *harj-o-marj* ('anarchy', 'disorder') and was subsequently declared to have been illegal. But the damage was already done. Fearing protracted lawsuits with little hope of a fair outcome, a great number of Western-educated teachers and scientists sought to leave Iran while they could. This resulted in an exodus which was one of the greatest disservices of the Islamic Revolution to the nation.

I tried unsuccessfully several times that summer to gain an exit permit to enable me to go to England for a few weeks. Although merely requiring an official stamp on a piece of paper, I never seemed to get past the minions at the lower end of academic bureaucracy. I decided to try one last time, but on this occasion I asked to see the Chancellor in person on a personal matter. As luck would have it he was absent from his office that day, and sitting in his place behind the ornate desk was a youngish, bespectacled official who informed me that he had been appointed as the Chancellor's deputy, and he asked why I had come. I replied that I needed the Chancellor's approval to allow me to go to London to visit my aunt, and presented the sheet of paper with my request. The deputy looked me in the eye and asked whether there was any reason I should not be allowed to leave. I hesitated, then confessed that I had apparently been declared *matrood,* but I wasn't really sure why. 'Oh, is that all?' exclaimed the deputy. 'Everyone in the country is now *matrood!* My brother and uncle have just been told they're *matrood*—it doesn't mean a thing anymore!' And with those words he slid open a drawer, took out a tray of rubber stamps, and, selecting one, proceeded to stamp my paper. 'There you are *Khânum,*' he said. 'Have a nice holiday!' I looked down at the exit permit in my hands which now had 'sanctioned' clearly printed across its heading. Thanking him politely I left the office, not quite believing it had been so easy. After weeks of frustration it seemed a minor miracle. Baba and Mami were a little more philosophical. They believed in *ghismat* ('destiny', anglicised as 'kismet')—it had been God's will all along that I should go to England. From that moment on they were reassured that my going was part of God's plan.

───◆───

Leaving for England this time around lacked the eager anticipation of eight years previously. This time I felt apprehensive to be going because I was unsure of what the future had in store. Religious persecution was becoming ever more rampant in Tehran. Even Jews and Zoroastrians who had been tolerated for centuries were coming under increasing scrutiny. Proof of Armenian or Assyrian origin in the form of an identity card was even sometimes required at overtly public Christian gatherings. As a family we felt that the longer I remained at home, the greater would be the likelihood that I would somehow get into trouble. Besides, I had no job, and no husband, and sadly no immediate prospects. Perhaps I had become too *farangi* for Iran.

With my exit permit finally secured, I booked my flight to London. Ostensibly I was just going away for the summer and I had a return date on my ticket. However, in reality I was going away to see if I could secure employment as a Student Nurse in England. If I were successful and stayed the course, we were all certain that in three years' time when I qualified, the country would be back to normal and that I would return. Normality was what we craved above all else, even though Baba believed he would not live long enough to see it. The chaos and bloodshed of the subsequent Iran-Iraq war was to prove him to be correct.

~❦~

On the day of my departure Tehran airport was teeming with guards and would-be security militia. The terminal was jammed with people. Entire families had gathered to say goodbye to their loved ones, perhaps for the last time, and many were distraught. I had encased my head and shoulders very modestly in a large scarf so as not to draw attention to myself, but my main worry was that my passport would be withheld at security and I would be denied travel. Baba and Mami accompanied me to the glass doors of the departure gate. There, in the midst of teeming humanity, we said our farewells. At the very last minute Mami shocked me by saying: 'Go and make a life for yourself. Try to be happy. And don't come back too soon!' Whatever I had thought was in her mind that day I certainly didn't think it was this. I can't imagine what drove her to say it, but I knew she had meant well. Baba said nothing but looked perturbed. It was a sobering moment. We said goodbye in the midst of that milling throng and they asked me to return to the departure gate once I had secured my passport so that they would know I had made it through security. Over the din we heard my flight being announced, and I stepped forward to join the queue of departing passengers.

To my utter relief my passport was handed to me without any questions and I was simply waved through. I could see Baba and Mami standing together behind the tall glass doors. In the mêlée they appeared insignificant—small, old, and grey, like two injured sparrows. I felt a sudden pang. Should I really be going? What if something happened to them while I was away? But the die was cast. I waved to them from the turnstiles, holding my passport aloft. They saw me and waved back, their faces now wreathed in smiles, and I turned away and followed the other passengers into the departure lounge.

On the IranAir flight everyone sat in complete silence. I had a window seat, and looking down as we circled over Tehran, the city looked desolate, like an adobe-coloured Dresden after it had been bombed. Clay-brown buildings, many roofless, stretched for miles. There wasn't a blade of grass to be seen anywhere. In a wasteland, dozens of grounded Bell helicopters rusted away, having been abandoned to the ravages of desert sand. When the pilot announced that we had cleared Iranian airspace, the entire cabin erupted in a loud frenzy of clapping and rejoicing. Women began to divest themselves of their *châdors* and scarves, and some even began to apply lipstick and make-up while still strapped in their seats. A queue of ladies formed for the washrooms, emerging one by one having transformed themselves into *farangi* lookalikes.

⁂

In London I was greeted warmly by my jolly Aunt Mehri who was Baba's stepsister and younger than him by some twenty years. As an unmarried girl she had lived with us in Geneva for a while when I was very young but I had not seen her for many years. We made our way to their home in the suburbs where I was welcomed by David, her doctor husband, and by their three young sons who were my half-English cousins. The British immigration authorities had stamped my passport with an entry permit valid for six weeks. It didn't leave much time to sort out any future plans.

I decided that the quickest course of action would be to go in person straight to the top. After completing the relevant St George's Hospital Application for Nurse Training form, I took this, with a copy of my *curriculum vitae*, to the Head of Nurse Training Recruitment at their new premises in the Tooting area of south London. Mr Mullen, the newly appointed nursing recruitment officer, glanced at the application and read my CV while I sat before him. Then, fixing me with his steely blue eyes, he said:

'I see that you have come with a glowing reference from the Matron at Notre Dame de Fatima Hospital in Tehran, and I also see that you would cope well academically with the rigours of nurse training. Nevertheless I must disappoint you. Given your background, frankly I don't believe you'll stay the course. I need dependable nurses to staff the hospital. You've moved around a great deal, and you're presently in Britain only on a temporary visa. I simply can't afford to offer you training and then have you leave us. I'm afraid it's a "No".'

Devastated, I pleaded my case with an eloquence I didn't know I possessed. I begged him to give me a chance. I said I would apply for an extension of the visa, I would work during the holidays, I was mature, I was dependable, I was a quick learner, most patients preferred to be cared for by older nurses.... I did everything I could, short of standing on my head, to convince this recruitment god. Mr Mullen hesitated. Then, perhaps mindful that his big, new hospital needed nurses urgently, he said: 'OK, I'll accept you. But remember, you'll be an NHS employee and this government isn't made of money. I don't want you coming back to knock on my door in a few months' time asking to leave!'

I was ecstatic! Signing on the dotted line bound me to the United Kingdom National Health Service for a minimum of three years. I would begin training to be nurse in a few weeks' time, be given a room in the Nurses' Home, and awarded a meagre salary. Back at Aunt Mehri's, we celebrated my victory around the kitchen table. My youngest cousin informed me while he was sad to see me go to live in the hospital, he was glad to be getting his bedroom back!

Nowadays British nurses train through universities and students are supernumerary to the workforce until they qualify. But until the 1980s nurse training in the United Kingdom was through individual 'Teaching Hospitals', and both Student and Enrolled Nurses were employed on the wards as junior staff. As they advanced in seniority and commensurately in responsibilities, so their salaries incrementally increased. This was how I was able to support myself financially. It would not have been possible for me a decade later as I was already a graduate and wouldn't have qualified for another bursary—I happened to have been in the right place at the right time.

At the Immigration Centre in Croydon, my Iranian passport with its now obsolete 'Empire of Iran' ensign still emblazoned on its cover was stamped with a permission to enter the United Kingdom for the duration of my nursing course with the *proviso* that this would be reviewed annually by the Immigration Aliens' Office. I now had a student visa and was given an Aliens' Registration Number. Aliens' Registration rules required me to report every year to the Aliens' Office of a British constabulary to confirm my details and current place of abode. Officially I was now 'safe' for a while. I just prayed that I wouldn't discover that I hated nursing!

⚜

In fact I found that actually liked nursing. Almost like a repeat of Nottingham when I had been an older postgraduate among undergraduates, I was now a mature student, aged nearly thirty, in a cohort of mostly school-leavers. Although this gave me the edge with hospital patients for whom life's experiences count for something, I was less well equipped than my peers with recent school honours in human biology. Additionally, all the other young student nurses seemed to be completely at home with naked bodies of both sexes. My prudish upbringing did me no favours on my first hospital ward, which was Male Surgical. A steep learning curve ensued over which I will draw an obligatory veil. Nevertheless, I found that I loved both the hierarchy and the orderliness of hospital routines—so refreshingly different from my familiarity with both the isolation the ivory tower of Literature and the recent *harj-o-marj* of Tehran.

We First Year Student Nurses were distinguished from the other students by our white belts and our caps which had a single blue stripe. We looked up to our Second Year peers whose belts were light blue and whose caps had two stripes, and to the Final Years who had royal blue belts and caps with three stripes; and we were in absolute awe of State Registered Nurses with their white elasticated arm cuffs and frilly starched caps. Ward Sisters ran their Nightingale-style wards with iron-clad authority. Woe betide any nurse who came on duty with her cap aslant, or a wisp of hair escaping, or a hole in her black lisle stockings! When Sister spoke, you answered with your hands behind you back: 'Yes Sister,' 'No Sister,' 'Three-bags-full, Sister.' Surnames only were used—the use of familiar first names was deemed unprofessional. It was always 'Nurse Smith' or 'Nurse McKinnon'—never 'Susan' or 'Beth'. My surname *Hafezi* was unusual, but I still wasn't best pleased to have it pronounced it as *Hafeeeezi* which led to endless jokes about *Nurse Half-Easy*!

Only marginally more senior than the nursing auxiliaries, we junior students were the cleaning backbone of the hospital wards. Not for us the holistic nursing model of Total Patient Care which would be introduced a decade later. The regime then was well and truly Task Orientated. As First Years we cleaned and cleaned and cleaned! Every day every single patient's bedside locker and bed frame, including each one of its four wheels, was scrubbed with antiseptic; beds made up with fresh sheets; specimen and denture pots washed out; jugs of drinking water replaced; and patients' flowers re-arranged. We learned to make beds in a particular nurse-savvy way with sheets that displayed 'hospital corners' (except that ours were folded in a superior way and called 'St George's Corners'). Under Sister's eagle eye, we were taught to look after our patients' every physical need in the methodical and kindly manner of nursing's greatest innovator, Florence Nightingale. We were often upbraided publicly for any minor inattention to detail. It was quite galling to be openly criticised for not swabbing down a stainless steel trolley in the 'approved' manner, and there were always several First Years in tears behind the scenes, hiding in the Ward Sluice. Such occasions fostered a team-spirited bond between us which stood the test of time. In 2014, there was a thirty-five year reunion of our 1979 Nurses' Set at St George's Hospital in Tooting. Almost everyone from our original group travelled to London for the occasion, many of us now grey-haired and edging towards retirement. It was a fitting tribute to the close bonds we had formed aeons earlier as green juniors on Male Surgical.

I settled well into the routine of hospital life. I didn't stick out much as an oddity; I had no hang-ups about being far from home, or indeed of being the oldest in my Set. I even coped with having to learn the dreaded biology in my spare time. I can only recall a single incident which belied my recent circumstances. A few months into training, I was on a Late Shift on Bonfire Night. (For the benefit of non-British readers, Bonfire Night commemorates an incident which occurred in London on 5th November 1605 when Guy Fawkes, a Catholic revolutionary, plotted to blow up the Houses of Parliament along with the Protestant King James I of England. He was discovered with barrels of gunpowder and publicly burned to death on a pyre. This event is commemorated every year by firework displays and the burning of effigies of 'the guy' on a bonfire.) On that particular evening, peace was suddenly shattered by loud bangs as fireworks and brilliant rockets exploded outside and flashes of light appeared at our ward windows. In a single instant, and without thinking, I immediately dived under the nearest patient's bed and crouched there hugging my knees with my head bent down and my cap knocked askew. Nobody else moved or joined me. After a few moments I saw Sister's face peering at me over the side of the bed frame. '*Nurse Hafeeeeezi!* Come out of there at once! What is the meaning of this unseemly behaviour?' When I sheepishly explained that I had thought we were being bombed—an instinctive reaction in someone who had recently lived through months of explosions in Tehran—she was slightly mollified, but nevertheless lectured me quite firmly on the professional virtue of controlling one's natural impulses whilst on duty!

I could recount many incidents, some of them quite comical, that happened to me during my first year as a student nurse, but such stories could fill an entire book, so reluctantly I will stop here.

Christmas 1979 was approaching. I already knew I would be on duty on Christmas Day but I had Christmas Eve free. I was no longer the naïve student I had been in Nottingham in what seemed a lifetime ago. I had friends and colleagues. I was acquainted with fellow worshippers in the local Anglican parish. I even had relatives nearby in Aunt Mehri and her family. I decided that this year I would plan ahead and do the *farangi* thing and send Christmas cards to my friends from Nottingham days whose addresses I had preserved in an old address book. As I flipped through its alphabetical pages I came to the letter 'R' with James's details. We had had no contact whatsoever with each other for almost three years, and for all I knew James had moved on and was now probably married with children. I was under no illusion that our relationship was now well and truly over, but not a single day had passed since we had parted without my asking God to give him grace and happiness—because deep down I secretly still loved him and knew that I always would. I debated whether or not to write. In the end I sent a brief note saying that I was back in England and living in London. I reckoned that he had probably moved on from Nottingham, and I didn't expect a reply.

To my surprise an envelope arrived not long afterwards addressed to me in a familiar hand. It was postmarked 'Paisley, Renfrewshire, Scotland'. My letter had been forwarded from Nottingham to his parents in Warwickshire, and they had forwarded it to his current address in Glasgow. In a brief message, James gave a Glasgow telephone number and said he hoped I might call. It was mainly curiosity that drove me to do so. In those pre-mobile-phone days I had to use a public telephone, which in the Nurses' Home was wall-mounted in the main corridor beside the staircase. Our conversation, which could be overheard by anyone passing, went something like this:

F: Hello?
J: Hello. What are you doing in London?
F: I'm a training to be a nurse. What are you doing in Glasgow?
J: *Really?* I'm a Registrar in Orthopaedic surgery on the Glasgow Western Surgical Rotation—it includes Paisley.
F: Really? That's nice. Are you married?
J: No. Are you?
F: No.

LONG SILENCE

J: Come to Glasgow and visit me some time—I'm in a two-bedroom flat.
F: That sounds nice—I might.

After this conversation my heart was all a-flutter. 'Get a grip!' I told myself firmly. 'It's *over.*' I debated the pros and cons of a potential meeting, and in the end my not always very wise 'leap first and ask questions later' mentality won over. The Nurses' Duty Roster, which was pinned onto our student nurses' notice-board, indicated that following a ten-day stretch of duty I would have four days off in the middle of the month. Because I was curious to see where James lived, and because I had never been to Scotland before, I decided to go to Glasgow during those few days—it would be an adventure—after which we would hopefully part amicably and each move on with our respective lives.

Our wedding day, St Leonard's Church, Nottingham, 17ᵗʰ May 1980

Chapter 10

MARRIAGE

As the train drew north out of Euston Station I gazed out of the window and wondered what the next few days might bring. Three years had elapsed and we were now both older and had led very different lives in that time. I didn't want the bubble with the memory of what had been between us to burst. On the other hand, like a moth inexorably drawn towards a flame, I could not let this opportunity pass. The scenery outside gradually became wilder and more windswept and soon we were north of Carlisle and into the Scottish Borders. Here the landscape was rolling hills, wooded valleys and fields full of sheep—countryside that had inspired Burns and Scott. Iran and its political woes seemed a world away.

James was standing on the platform at Glasgow Central. I spotted him immediately—there was no mistaking the tall distinguished looks, the familiar kindly smile, and the soft wave of brown hair. His face was slightly more lined than I remembered, and the hands that clasped mine felt dry from hours of surgical scrubbing. James lived in a flat on the top floor of a house in the middle of a Victorian terrace. Athole Gardens was bordered by stone tenement buildings on three sides, each with a back drying green, and a terrace of Victorian houses on the remaining sides. The mature gardens in the centre of the square were enclosed by ornate iron railings and the proprietors of all the flats were supplied with a key to its gate. Number 41, where James lived, had originally housed a single family plus servants. It had been converted into four flats: a 'garden flat' in the basement, two larger ones on the ground and first floors, each with a grand bay window overlooking the street, and a smaller flat in the attic area which was James's apartment.

As we stepped up to the entrance of the house, I saw the lace curtains in the front bay window twitch. 'That's Mrs Blair who lives downstairs,' James informed me. 'Mrs B keeps an eye on all our comings and goings, and she's especially inquisitive about "The Young Doctor Upstairs"!' The attic flat had the high ceilings and cornices which grace so many of the grand Glasgow stone terraces. It had a small galley kitchen, a bathroom with an enormous bathtub, and two bedrooms, one of which served as James's study. The cosy book-lined sitting room had tall windows overlooking a back lane and the modest workshop premises of the well-known Saltoun Pottery. In pride of place was an old upright piano which James had bought with money given to him by his parents to buy a bed. James had bought the piano instead—it was a real bargain, apparently.

Athole Gardens, Glasgow (no.41 is the middle house in this row)

At first we were both inordinately polite and the atmosphere felt a little awkward. I feared it was going to be a long weekend. I stood in the kitchen while James put the kettle on and removed a casserole from the refrigerator. 'It's our dinner,' he said by way of explanation. I lifted the lid and noted its appetising contents. 'That looks like a nice stew,' I commented politely. '"*Stew*"?' he expostulated. 'Are you calling my very best daube de boeuf à la provençale a "*stew*"?' I've just spent two whole days slaving over this recipe!' We looked at each other in silence, then we both simultaneously burst out laughing—and the ice was well and truly broken.

That weekend was a success—completely magical. We ate the delicious meal which showed off James's culinary prowess, and talked far into the night. I spoke about life in Tehran and what had happened in the Revolution. James was intrigued that I had re-invented myself as a Student Nurse. With his intimate knowledge of the hospital world he said I definitely wouldn't find it 'a walk in the park'. Meanwhile, he had passed the FRCS (Fellow of the Royal College of Surgeons) examinations and was now training in orthopaedic surgery. Having recently secured a Registrar post in Glasgow his aim was to specialise in paediatric orthopaedic surgery. He said he was permanently tired from all the on-call hours. Working 120 hours at a stretch every week was then not unknown among junior doctors, and it left very little time for socialising.

When it was time for me to leave, we decided that we would meet again. However, we were now five hundred miles apart, and both working punishing hospital shifts. Because of James's onerous 'on-call' duties, it would be easier for me to come up to Glasgow. Student nurses' rotas at St George's Hospital had been allocated ahead for the three years of our training schedule on a mammoth Nursing Planner. While there was little leeway in terms of the ability to change anything, I could predict my days off and annual leave allocation until the very end of training. Besides, there was a spare bedroom at James's place, whereas he couldn't stay in the Nurses' Home.

For a delightful few weeks that late autumn we managed some weekends together, mostly spent in long conversations, walking along the Clyde riverbank, visiting art galleries, and listening to the classical music which we both loved. I hoped our sporadic meetings would continue for a long time. But just when I was enjoying this new chapter, James came up with a suggestion that was a bolt from the blue:

'I don't think we should carry on like this indefinitely—travelling huge distances to meet up every so often, and then both of us being on our best behaviour. If this relationship is ever going to work I suggest we test it by going away on holiday together to see whether we still like each other at close quarters.' He had obviously given the situation a fair amount of thought and had come to the conclusion that living together for a fortnight would give some indication of long-term compatibility within a short space of time.

I was taken aback by this suggestion and initially quite reluctant. For starters, I didn't think I would be able to stand it if the holiday didn't work out and we fell out for some reason. Secondly, my puritanical upbringing didn't give me the licence to go away on holiday with lone men, no matter how innocent the sleeping arrangements. If the rumour mill started rolling it would spell social death for me back home. On the other hand, I could see some sense in it—neither of us was keen to waste the best years of our lives in an unresolved relationship, and we needed to find out once and for all whether or not we were really meant for each other. James's idea was that somewhere culturally interesting would provide a fall-back option for both of us to enjoy the break even if we decided that our relationship would go no further. His suggestion was North Africa—only a few hours' flight from London, warm in December, with spoken French as an added bonus.

Eventually I came round to acknowledging it was a good idea, but what on earth would Baba and Mami say? I found it difficult to throw off the mantle of my strictly insular Middle Eastern upbringing which frowned on liaisons before marriage. In the end I went to Aunt Mehri about my dilemma. She told me in no uncertain terms to stop dithering! She said the entire family knew I had carried a secret flame for this man for years. Now the same man who seemed to be a decent sort was asking to get to know me a little better—surely the sensible thing was to say yes.

'What about losing my *âberu* (dignity)?' I hazarded.

'Your *âberu* is within you,' said Aunt Mehri. 'It's the way you lead in your life—not what others think of you. Besides you're no longer young—how many more years of your life are you going to waste stringing this romance along? Go and book the blinking holiday right now, and find out once and for all whether he's the man for you!' Then she added as an afterthought, 'And for God's sake, don't ever tell your Baba that I encouraged you to go on some jaunt with a *farangi* man—he'd kill me!'

I decided I would go. I didn't give my parents all the details—I just wrote saying that I had booked a coach tour of cities in Morocco during my upcoming annual leave with a group of people, 'some of whom' I knew well. This wasn't the entire truth, but the last thing I wanted now was a letter arriving from Iran forbidding me to go! 'Cosmos' was the firm which arranged our itinerary, billed as the 'Jewels of Morocco'. It included a week-long coach tour of the cities of Casablanca, Rabat, Marrakech, Fez, and Meknes, plus another week on the south coast at Agadir. I prayed that I would not return from this trip with the door closed on our friendship. I knew I was taking a risk. It's eminently possible to hide one's less attractive personal habits when living apart—not so easy at close quarters. I had heard enough salutary tales about longstanding friendships breaking up after a holiday in the sun and I didn't want to end up as another casualty.

⁓⁂⁓

On a cold, drizzly day in mid-December, James came down to London and we flew to Casablanca, a dazzling white city bathed in glorious sunshine. On arrival we both spoke effortlessly in French with our tour guide and coach driver, instantly impressing the handful of British tourists who were our coach companions. We discovered a mutual fondness for the Arabic fare on offer and were quite content to sit outside ramshackle street cafés to sample the local *tagine* followed by a glass of mint tea, rather than to follow our less-discerning fellow travellers in search of beer, egg and chips.

Strolling out on the seafront promenade in the evening we were amused when a few Maghrebi women turned to look at me somewhat accusingly as if to say: 'That local girl has nabbed herself a tourist!' I suppose my looks probably resembled theirs and they took me for a native Moroccan. We watched the harbour slowly come to life under twinkling stars and a large golden moon hanging just above the crested waves where fishing boats bobbed up and down. Casablanca was a beguiling place.

We saw a lot of Morocco from our coach during that first week. The souks and alleyways of ancient cities like Marrakesh and Fez were fascinating, bursting with Maghrebi mystique, complementing the surrounding serene countryside and Atlas Mountains, home to the nomadic Berbers. Fez medina well-deserves its World Heritage accolade, as does the Djema-al-F'na in Marrakesh with its biblical street atmosphere. A surprising discovery was that of the well-preserved ruins of the ancient Roman city of Volubilis on the road between Rabat and Meknes. We were fortunate to be visiting this country in the late 'seventies before the package holiday industry fully took off, with the advent of highrise hotels and coach parks.

In each other's company during the long days spent in the coach, James and I seemed to fit together like a hand and a glove. We were supremely happy simply to be together, exactly as we were, and not seeking anything in return. It felt just wonderful. By the time we arrived in the southern city of Agadir for what was to be the second part of the holiday, we both knew that something had subtly changed—though neither of us voiced it aloud.

Agadir is on the Atlantic coast with a warm and balmy climate. It was completely flattened by an earthquake as recently as 1960 and rebuilt with tourism in mind as a seaside resort. At the time we went it boasted only a few modest beachfront hotels, one of which was the Al-Moghar, where we were billeted. Even in December we were able to swim in the sea and sit in the sun. We strolled in the palm-fringed gardens at sunset, and walked into town in the evenings. It was completely idyllic.

On Christmas Eve, knowing how important it was for me, James took me to the only church in town, Sainte Anne, for *la Messe Solonelle de Minuit* which was celebrated in French. The church was packed with tourists, French residents and Christian Arabs. On Christmas morning we sat on the sand at the water's edge watching the Atlantic rollers crashing on the surf. The beach was completely deserted except for a lone camel and its keeper who tried valiantly to sell us a woollen Berber-style blanket. The conversation between this man and James, conducted entirely in French, whereby James informed the hawker that he had come from Scotland which is the homeland of woollen blankets, was hilarious.

We were due to fly back the day after Boxing Day. In the New Year, James would leave Paisley to join the surgical team at Glasgow's Royal Hospital for Sick Children. I was also due to move wards at St George's—from Male Surgical to Female Medical, and I hoped that my new rota would be flexible enough to allow visits to Glasgow.

James had other ideas altogether.

———※———

On our last day in Agadir we were relaxing in a secluded part of the Al-Moghar, when out of the blue James took my hand and asked me whether I would consider marrying him and becoming his wife. I was so overcome with emotion that I could hardly breathe! Of course I said 'Yes' without a moment's hesitation. The exquisite intensity of that moment completely overwhelmed us both.

Afterwards I needed to be alone. I meandered through the gardens and sat down beneath a shady cypress to thank God. I didn't deserve such a perfect outcome from a trip I almost hadn't taken. I had been dilatory in accepting Christ's call over many years. And despite the promise '...seek ye first the kingdom of

God...and all these things shall be added unto you' (*Matthew* 6:33), I knew I was unworthy of being given my heart's desire, and was quite inarticulate in my gratitude. But in the distance I saw James waiting for me, and he had such a wonderful smile on his face that he looked almost ten years younger. It was truly the happiest moment of my life.

⊱✦⊰

As soon as we returned from our trip, James wrote to my father asking formally for my hand in marriage. We awaited Baba's response before making any announcements: 'We owe it to him,' he said. 'Your father must be the first to know.' It was just six months since I had left Iran and only three since James and I had met again. James's friends said they knew he was a cautious man—definitely not someone would leap in where angels feared to tread—but, *Boy*, could the man move when he wanted to!

We decided to get married in Nottingham. Iran was out of the question and neither of us presently had a real attachment either to London or to Glasgow. Nottingham was where we had first met, and it had once been a second home to me. We would ask Douglas Davies who had introduced us to conduct our marriage service. 'He may as well finish off what he started!' James quipped. I asked Marion, my old friend from F Floor in Willoughby Hall, to be my bridesmaid. A few friends thought our choice of venue was crazy:

'You're in London, James is in Glasgow, his parents are in Warwickshire, Marion is in Belfast, your mum and dad are in Tehran—why on earth are you getting married somewhere else altogether?' It did sound slightly mad, but it made sense to us. In terms of where we should live afterwards, it would be Glasgow. I decided to complete my nursing course but to transfer training to Scotland. During these discussions I reminded James that he had once emphatically declared that he would never marry a nurse—it has now become an oft-repeated family joke!

James said he would speak to Douglas while I sorted out my

~ 186 ~

transfer to Scotland. I was delighted to be informed quite soon that our wedding would take place in just a few months' time, on 17th May 1980, at St Leonard's Anglican Church in Nottingham where Douglas was priest. We would need a Special Licence to marry there as neither of us lived within its parish. I was particularly keen to have the Eucharist celebrated at our marriage. It was massively important for me to have Christ tangibly present at this most solemn moment in our lives. James acquiesced, though he did say it wasn't commonly the done thing. There would be the problem of guests not wishing to partake the Communion either because they belonged to a different denomination, or because they felt unprepared; and there would be others, like my parents and Aunt Mehri, who weren't Christians. Douglas found the perfect solution: 'We'll celebrate Holy Communion just for the two of you, as an adjunct to your marriage vows. That way no one will feel left out and it will sanctify the occasion in a very special way.'

Religion had been the single most important subject which we discussed at length before our marriage. Despite his tongue-in-cheek remarks about how he had potentially rescued me from a life in the convent, James knew how seriously I took my faith. Religion hadn't been an important aspect of his own early home life. James's parents were observant but not particularly religious. His father was a Scottish Presbyterian and his mother a member of the Dutch Reformed Church of South Africa. James had been received into the Methodist Church, but had rather too much religion in his adolescent years. He remains sympathetic towards Christianity, but prefers to keep spiritual matters to himself. While James's faith is not all-consuming in the same way that it is for me, he did give me his solemn promise that he would always support me in that respect. And he has kept that promise. However, he was equally adamant that he would always remain completely honest about his own beliefs and never pretend to be something he wasn't. I could not have asked for more.

With our all-important day planned and the Special Licence applied for, I fastened my treasured engagement ring with a safety pin to the inside of the pocket of my nurse's uniform and tripped gaily down the 'management wing' of St George Hospital to where the administrative offices were located. I stood for a moment outside the polished door with its salient plaque inscribed 'ASST. MATRON', and in smaller letters 'Mr A Mullen / Recruitment Office'. Smoothing down my uniform and making sure no wisps of hair were escaping from beneath my cap, I knocked. 'Come in!' said a voice, and I put my head round the door. Mr Mullen was standing under a large framed painting of Florence Nightingale. As soon as he saw me, he frowned, and thumping his fist on the mahogany desk, he exclaimed,

'Nurse *Hafeeeeezi?* I knew it! You're not staying with us are you? You've come to tell me you're leaving!'

'Oh, but I'm not leaving the profession,' I said boldly, standing tall. 'I still want to be a nurse. It's just that I'm getting married soon, and I would like to request a transfer of training hospitals.'

'Oh, so you're getting married now, are you? That was quick work—you don't seem to have been here that long! And who, may I ask, is the lucky man?'

I recounted the saga of our relationship which I had rehearsed beforehand to ensure it sounded reasonably coherent and dispelled any notion of a shotgun wedding. I also emphasised that my fiancé was a National Health Service surgeon currently working his fingers to the bone. As he listened to my ramble, I noted Mr Mullen's expression softening slightly. After I had finished, he sighed.

'OK, we're not dragons here at St George's, if you'll pardon my pun; and since you say you're determined to continue as nurse I'll see about getting you transferred to the Western Infirmary in Glasgow—they have a good reputation.' By now my face was wreathed in smiles.

'Mind you,' he continued, 'the Scots will exact a price—this is an exception to the rule, and you'll have to pay the penalty for swapping Area Health Authorities during training, which means you will have to work an extra three months for Greater Glasgow Health Board before you can be fully qualified as a State Registered Nurse. The NHS has to guard against setting a precedent of student nurses wanting to up-sticks and move around the country during training... if we're not careful there'll soon be a bunch of Janes and Mollys all requesting to move because of family circumstances.'

I realised that this would mean that I would be in my mid-thirties before I finally qualified, but I was so happy that I could almost have kissed Mr Mullen!

During one of my weekends off when I wasn't catching the train to Glasgow to be with James, Aunt Mehri and I went shopping in London for my wedding gown. Afterwards we went to a modest tea room near the department store. It was the last time I had the opportunity for a decent conversation with this jolly aunt who was Baba's youngest step-sibling. Of course Aunt Mehri took all the credit for the fact that James and I were at last going to be wed—after all, it was she who had advised me to go on holiday with him in the first place. Although I had hardly known her previously, we discovered we had a lot in common and, given the opportunity, we could have become very close. Mehri had also trained as a nurse in London and had married a British doctor, a marriage which was a success despite having had to learn *farangi* ways from scratch as her early life had been lived in Semnan.

'You're better equipped for marriage in this country than I was,' she said. 'You're practically British already.' Aunt Mehri then regaled me with stories of her early married life in London in the 'sixties and of how ill-prepared she had been for housewifely duties as there had always been an army of women in her childhood home who had done all the cooking and cleaning. Apparently she had once nearly served up a dish of chopped and fried tulip bulbs having assumed that they were onions! I treasure the memory of that conversation as bittersweet because my aunt also confided that she was currently being treated for the recurrence of cancer following removal of one of her breasts a few years previously in the United States. It was a real tragedy. She was only forty years old and their youngest child only ten. Unfortunately, we only met a few more times after that occasion, and I'll always regret that I didn't get a chance to have a proper chat with her on our wedding day, when, unbeknown to us, she had only three months left to live.

A delighted Baba and Mami managed to acquire exit permits to come to England for the wedding and had booked their IranAir flight to London to arrive exactly one week beforehand. That week would be spent meeting and getting to know their future son-in-law. They knew I was very happy, but the additional knowledge that James was a doctor and that his father had been a bank manager seemed equally important. I would have married James if he had been a dustman, but to Baba and Mami professional status meant a great deal. I remember that Baba's first question to me whenever I introduced a new friend had always been: 'And what does her/his father do for a living?'

We had arranged that immediately after the wedding, Baba and Mami would leave with James's parents and stay with them for a few days before returning home to Tehran. James and I would spend our first night together in a country inn not far away, and arrive in time for lunch the next day. We felt it would not be right for us to disappear on honeymoon without a proper goodbye.

In early March 1980, six weeks before the all-important date, I heard on the BBC radio channel that new, stricter visa regulations were going to be enforced for Iranians entering the United Kingdom. Until then, reciprocal arrangements between our two countries meant that Iranian passport holders could come to Britain and be given leave to enter as tourists without a visa. That was to stop and visas would now be required. The date set for the enforcement of this new regulation was announced as 17th May. 'Hang on a minute,' I thought, 'that's our wedding day!' It dawned on me that we were leaving for France on our honeymoon the day after getting married and not returning to the UK for a fortnight—would I be allowed back in the country without this new visa? I currently had a temporary student visa as well as an Alien's Registration number—surely that was sufficient? I would be entitled to apply for British citizenship after marriage, but until this was awarded, in British eyes I was an Iranian Alien. For the sake of clarification I thought it would be prudent to go to the UK Passport Office in London and enquire in person.

At the Passport Office I put my case forward.

'Yes, madam,' said the official. 'You will certainly need the new visa to re-enter the UK if you're returning to these shores after 17th May.'

'But that's the day I'm getting married—and it's a Saturday,' I said, knowing the Consulate would be closed, even if I could have conceivably hoofed it down to London and back in time to get married in Nottingham. 'We'll be going to France straight afterwards. Is there any way I can get this visa stamped in my passport before then?'

'I'm afraid not, madam,' said the official. 'The law only comes into force on 17th May, so the visa can't be issued until then. Your best bet would be to go to the British Embassy in Paris while you're in France and apply there for the visa before returning to the UK.'

I didn't think this would be at all convenient for we had already booked ahead several nights in various country hotels dotted round the Loire valley, in western France—nowhere near Paris. There seemed to be no end of complications to being an Iranian in *Farang*.

Baba and Mami duly arrived from Iran and we had an emotional reunion. They met their future *farangi* son-in-law, and of course James charmed their socks off, as I knew he would. Mami had been to a dressmaker in Tehran and had got a nice apricot-coloured outfit to wear for the occasion. At the last minute she had also purchased a *farangi* style hat which was little more than a fancy feathered affair. Because she didn't want it to get crushed during the journey, she had placed it inside the aluminium pan of the electric rice-cooker which was to have been our wedding present. But when she and Baba had arrived at Tehran airport they were informed that there was a ban on all electrical appliances leaving the country because of the West's current trade embargo on the import of electrical goods to Iran. The rice-cooker must be left behind. Mami reluctantly surrendered the large box to the airport customs official and she and Baba were allowed to proceed through the security checkpoint. It was only after their aeroplane had taken off from Tehran and they were flying over Turkey that she ruefully remembered her precious hat!

These were really only minor inconveniences. What was a real tragedy was the news of Bahram's murder in Tehran, which was aired on the BBC a few days before our wedding. Bishop Hassan had been away from Iran visiting his overseas flock in the Diocese of Cyprus when this happened. His wife Margaret was in Tehran caring for the Persian Church's diocesan secretary, Jean Waddell, who was recuperating in hospital having been recently shot by Islamist revolutionaries. Bahram failed to return home that evening. He had been accosted in his car after work, driven to an isolated country road and shot point blank in the head. No one was ever brought to justice for this terrible deed, and it was widely thought that the bullet that killed him was meant for his father, the Persian bishop. Alone in Nicosia, Bishop Hassan was informed his son's murder and due to post-revolutionary restrictions on travel he was unable to return to Iran. His wife was obliged to collect the body of their son on her own and take it back to Isfahan for a Christian burial. Bahram had been a good friend to me, a kind and intelligent young man with a bright future. His demise remains a sad and incalculable loss.

My last photo with Baba

Our wedding day dawned with plenty of spring sunshine. Baba, Mami and I were staying in the annexe of my old Hall — Willoughby. It was strange being back in the same dormitory where I had spent my student years. Willoughby Hall had moved with the times and was now co-educational with both male and female residents. As it was exam time there were a lot of undergraduates around. I remember being embarrassed by the crowd of students that had gathered outside the entrance to the Hall who clapped and cheered as I stepped out in my bridal gown and long veil carrying a bouquet of crimson roses while Baba and I waited for the car that would take us to St Leonard's

Church. Douglas had arranged a rehearsal beforehand so Baba knew exactly what to do at the ceremony. After he had handed me to James at the altar, he and Mami sat proudly in the front pew—their very first time at a Christian ceremony. Douglas preached a sermon on 'The Domestic Sacrament'. Receiving the consecrated Host and Chalice together with my new husband after Douglas had pronounced us man and wife was a moment of indescribable joy.

Together with our guests who, to my delight, included Johnny Graham, lately British Ambassador to Iran, as well as Stuart Burgess, Nottingham University's Methodist chaplain who had rescued me that very first Christmas, we all enjoyed a simple repast. Baba had declined to make the traditional father-of-the-bride's speech and had handed this task over to Aunt Mehri's husband. I don't remember what was said except that it included something about having to thank Ayatollah Khomeini for inciting the Revolution which had ultimately resulted in bringing us together. It caused a ripple of laughter, but Baba wasn't overly amused—like all Iranians he was anxious in case we were overheard and reported to a nameless authority.

Afterwards I changed out of my bridal gear with Marion's help, and after lots of thank yous and goodbyes James and I left in the same beaten-up car which he had owned ever since I had first met him. We were headed for a small country inn in the middle of a village not far from James's parents' home near Stratford-Upon-Avon. As we drove away showers of confetti began to blast into our faces from the car's air vents—apparently the work of Aunt Mehri's boys who had been secretly engaged in stuffing handfuls of it into the car's hidden corners. In fact, we were obliged to stop a few miles down the road to clear some of it out! The next morning James, who is by nature a very private person, was discomfited by the number of passers-by who were stopping to peer through his car windows at the confetti still strewn over the back seats while remarking loudly that the car belonged to 'those newly-weds staying at the Inn'!

We duly arrived at James's parents' house just before midday and found that Baba and Mami were being very well looked after. In fact both sets of parents had a number of interests in common, the main one being Bridge. Though they had not long met they had already been invited to stay an extra couple of days. I was really pleased about that. We had arranged this meeting to give us an opportunity to see my parents again, to thank them for everything, and to bid them a final goodbye. In her typical guileless fashion Mami enquired whether we had slept well, which made us blush to the roots of our hair. Then Baba took James aside and enjoined him to take good care of his daughter. Conversation was starting to get a little awkward, so it was a welcome relief when James's mother produced a magnificent lunch.

Signing the Register (Rev Douglas Davies is on my left)

Soon it was time for us to leave. We had a ferry booking for that evening's sailing from Portsmouth to Normandy. Saying goodbye to Baba and Mami wasn't easy, but it was a much happier leave-taking than our previous one barely a year ago at Tehran airport. At the last minute Baba slipped an envelope into my pocket which I later discovered contained French francs—a typically thoughtful gesture. As we drove off I looked back and waved at my parents until they were mere specks in the distance.

At last we were alone, able to unwind, and to delight in our union. Standing on the deck of the cross-channel ferry that evening with my husband's arms wrapped around me, his chin resting lightly on the top of my head, we watched the twinkling lights of the English shore slowly receding from view. The words of Ruth, the Moabite, came into my mind, and I silently made them my own:

> ...whither thou goest, I will go; and where thou lodgest, I will lodge; thy people will be my people, and thy God my God.

> *(Book of Ruth, 1:16)*

Our children, Edinburgh, 1994
(left to right: Alice, Mary, Laura, Andrew)

Chapter 11

MOTHERHOOD AND A SCOTTISH MULLAH

France in springtime is quite enchanting. We meandered slowly though the Loire valley admiring the heritage of its ancient town—Tours, Blois, Amboise, Orléans and the majestic architecture of the many *châteaux* nearby. On our second evening we stopped some two hundred kilometres south of Paris at La-Ferté-Saint-Aubin, a fortified hamlet deep in the heart of rural France. We were the sole guests in a modest *chambre d'hôte* and we were keen to sort out my visa situation before we went any further. The proprietor suggested that we drive north to Chartres and catch a train into Paris from there. We left the car near Chartres railway station and took the opportunity to visit the magnificent Gothic cathedral before boarding a local train for the centre of Paris.

Once there we made our way to the visa office of the British Consulate and were handed the relevant application forms to complete. In the corridor we encountered a knot of Iranian men bound for London who had been caught out by the new British visa requirement while transiting through Paris. They appeared to have very limited English and their French was non-existent. On realising that I was a compatriot who seemed to have no problem completing the forms they gathered round us and pleaded for help. I felt sorry for them and began to translate their documents, but our time was at a premium and I still had to get my own application processed. In the end I apologised lamely and with a few of the men still trailing hopefully after us, we made our way back to the visa office and were ushered in to see the Consul. The official took one cursory look at my application, and asked why I had left Britain. I explained that I had married the British subject who was standing right beside me, and I was keen to get back to Britain to resume my nursing course. The official leaned back in his chair with his eyes glazing over as though he had heard a similar tale many times before.

'How long have you been married?' he asked somewhat laconically.

'Three days, sir—we're presently on our honeymoon.'

The Consul's general demeanour immediately changed. He pulled himself upright in his chair and leaned over to shake James's hand. Then he called through to his colleague in the next office: 'Hey Fred, will you bring over some tea for this lady and gentleman!' And turning to us, he asked solicitously, 'You will have a cup of tea now, won't you? I'll get your visa sorted straight away…I am sorry that you've had to come so far to get it, but that's how things are at present, and the law is the law—even wives of British citizens must bow to British legislature!' We were quite happy to wait for the visa. Fred duly arrived bearing a tray laden with a bone china teapot, matching dainty cups and saucers, and a plate of Garibaldi biscuits. The Consul disappeared with my passport. We sat on the edge of our chairs and made polite small talk with Fred, a quintessential British civil servant wearing a natty bow tie and tweed jacket.

Alarmingly, angry raised voices were suddenly heard through the paper-thin office walls. The voices were speaking in a mixture of broken English and Persian, and the nameless folk were being given an extremely hard time trying to answer a volley of questions relating to immigration matters that was being barked at them. I guessed that they must be the group of Iranians we had come across in the corridor, and from the snatches we could hear I reckoned they were not going to get their visas easily. Fred appeared to be embarrassed at the clarity of the overheard conversation next door and relieved when his colleague reappeared with my passport, now stamped with the required visa. Thanking them for the tea we departed and left them to it. I still wonder whether that group of compatriots ever got to London, and I can't help feeling a little guilty at the ease with which I got mine. Language Is All, obviously.

Switching my nurse training to north of the Border and settling into married life in Glasgow was reasonably effortless, thanks mainly to the generosity and gregariousness of Glaswegians. By this time I had moved around enough countries to have acquired all the advantages of being a rolling stone, and had become adept in my role as a permanent foreigner. Of course, James's wide circle of friends and many cultural interests outside medicine made all the difference.

Mrs Blair from the downstairs flat recognised me instantly from all the occasions when she had kept an eye on my sporadic comings and goings from behind her lace curtains. She made a point of accosting me in our communal stairwell and confiding that she was glad James had finally made an honest woman of me—he worked far too hard and needed someone to look after him. 'Too right!' was James's only comment. He did work terribly long hours, and at times seemed to live permanently in the hospital. A few weeks after transferring to Glasgow I was allocated a fairly long stint of Night Duty and we became like ships passing in the night—James got out of bed in the morning and I got in… our bedroom curtains remained drawn for a whole month. Given that Mrs B had spread the word about the Young Doctor Upstairs getting himself a bride, our neighbours probably had a field day.

Glasgow folk are outgoing with none of the reserve typical of southerners. I was pleased to be able to start my new move as 'Nurse Robb' as it allayed the usual derogatory puns on the mispronunciation of my maiden name. My first nursing shift on the medical ward at Gartnavel Hospital was hilarious with some of the more mobile patients leaping out of their beds, the instant Sister's back was turned, to smoke clandestinely in the toilets, and others helpfully pushing linen trolleys around the ward and making sure I was doing my job right. I got attuned to *The Patter*, lingo unique to Glasgow, and quickly adopted a few useful nursing terms of my own: *wallies* (dentures). *stookie* (plaster cast) and *simmet* (vest). Sentences like the following appealed immensely to my earthy sense of humour: *Awa' an' bile yer heid* (stop talking nonsense), *O ba jings ah'm skunnered* (I'm very tired), and *Ah hav'nae a scooby, hen* (I've no idea, dear). I fell in love with Glasgow and felt very at home among its people. Although I now live in the more sedate rival city of Edinburgh, *Glassgeh* will always have a special place in my heart.

～❦～

One evening in early August when James was 'on-call' at the hospital, our doorbell rang. I wondered who it might be at that late hour, and opening the door I was shocked to see a policeman in full regalia standing on the stairs. He took out a little black notebook, and, licking the nib of his pencil, proceeded to flip over a few pages. I thought he was about to inform me that James had been run over by a bus and was currently lying unconscious and bleeding to death in a hospital. Why else would a police constable come to one's door at night? Visions of impending widowhood rose before my eyes, and for a moment I thought I would faint or be sick on the doorstep. 'Are you Farifteh Valentine Hafezi, citizen of Iran, date of birth 7th February 1950, entered the United Kingdom on 5th August 1979, lately living in London?'

I assented, and he continued lugubriously, 'Well, you didn't report your whereabouts to the Aliens Office yesterday. We managed to trace you to Scotland. Any reason why you didn't report?'

'Oh, is that all?' I said, flooded with relief. I had indeed forgotten the proviso of my initial entry permit. 'You see, I'm now married, and I've applied for British citizenship. I guess I just forgot.'

'You may have applied for British citizenship, madam,' said the bobby, 'and your application will be given due consideration. However, it is not yet a foregone conclusion, and despite having become the wife of a British subject, until such time as you receive a positive response from the Home Office regarding citizenship, your status remains that of an Alien. Kindly ensure that you report to the Aliens' Office of Greater Glasgow Constabulary in Sauchiehall Street forthwith.' I almost kowtowed in my relief at this anodyne request. After taking down my new surname and noting all James's details for good measure in his little black notebook, the policeman courteously doffed his crested constable's hat and bid me goodnight. I'm sure Mrs B was watching from her window and had not missed this intriguing night visitor!

Internet and electronic records have now made the whole process of such registrations much easier for everyone concerned. In accordance with Scottish law, when my naturalisation papers finally came through I was obliged to seek an appointment with a Justice of the Peace—in my case this was a retired judge—and to stand before him with one hand on a copy of the Bible reading the Oath of Allegiance to Queen and Country, after which he signed and witnessed my citizenship papers. Nowadays, this takes place in an official ceremony at the City Chambers, but in those days it was a much more intimate affair at the home of a Judge or a Scottish Sheriff.

⁓⊱⋆⊰⁓

In the summer of 1982 James was appointed Senior Registrar in orthopaedic surgery in Leeds, in West Yorkshire. Although I had completed my nurse training, I still had an extra three months before qualifying—my 'penalty' for swapping training hospitals. This meant that we lived apart for three months. James began his new job in Leeds staying in hospital accommodation while searching for somewhere for us to live; and I moved into the Nurses' Home in Glasgow after the sale of the flat in Athole Gardens. Yorkshire is not the easiest part of the country to access by rail from the west of Scotland, and getting our hospital shifts to synchronise was additionally difficult, so during those three long months we only managed a single weekend together.

Eventually James found an affordable semi-detached house in the Alwoodley area of Leeds, and with my new Registered General Nurse diploma under my belt I finally rejoined my husband and applied for a nursing post in one of Leeds's Teaching hospitals. I was fortunate to land a position on the Casualty Observation Ward at St James's University Hospital in Leeds—or 'Jimmy's' as it is locally known. This was 1982 and the notorious Yorkshire Ripper was believed to be still at large, terrorising women in Leeds and Bradford, haphazardly selecting his victims and bludgeoning them to death. Indeed his last victim had been a young hospital nurse on her way home after a night shift. In view of this, Matron who gave me my introductory tour of 'Jimmy's' also presented me with a personal alarm to activate in case I was apprehended. My face must have registered alarm, because she quickly said, 'I'm sure you understand—after all you've come from Glasgow where folk walk about with cut-throat razors in their back pockets!' I was obliged to inform her that this image of Glasgow was not one with which I was familiar.

My first day in the new post was a real struggle. I felt absolutely dreadful all day long—bone-tired and nauseous. I'm afraid I didn't make a great impression on my new nursing colleagues. I thought I was coming down with a dreaded lurgy, and had perhaps overdone the packing and unpacking of boxes, to say nothing of the stress of a recent job interview. When I returned home that evening I just fell into bed amid all the half-unpacked boxes and distempered walls, leaving James to a solitary dinner of tinned sardines and cold baked beans. Yes, you may have guessed—I was pregnant!

Within two years we were blessed with two lovely daughters, born within just a year of each other, and baptized at Alwoodley Methodist Church. Because of my difficult-to-pronounce-and-spell names we chose to give them simple ones. Our eldest is Alice (her name incorporates that of Baba's father 'Ali') and our second daughter is Mary (the anglicised version of 'Mehri'). When they were one and two years old respectively, James went to work for an orthopaedic surgeon in the Isère region of southeast France, at the Centre Hôpitalier de Grenoble, and we all moved there for a year. It was a wonderful time both in terms of work and work/life balance—a period we both remember with tremendous affection.

We lived in Leeds for nearly five years, one of which was spent in France. In 1987 James was appointed Consultant in Orthopaedic Surgery in Edinburgh. His field of expertise was paediatric orthopaedics, and in time he would become the senior orthopaedic surgeon at Edinburgh's Royal Hospital for Sick Children specialising in the orthopaedic management of children with cerebral palsy.

I was pregnant again, and our third daughter, Laura, was born exactly one month after we had moved back to Scotland. To all intents and purposes our family was now complete. By this time I had left nursing to be a mum at home. We didn't have any close family nearby—James's parents (Ouma and Oupa) were elderly and lived in England, his unmarried sister lived in Spain, and of course I had no immediate family in Scotland. I felt quite alone whenever I went into hospital to give birth, with no female companion to hold my hand or to mop my brow, as is always the case among Persian women in labour. While James was out providing for our family, I stayed home and looked after the children. Baba and Mami had managed one brief visit to Leeds, but that was the last time I saw Baba—he was now too old to travel.

～✦～

Readers can be forgiven in assuming that I have been blessed with inordinate optimism, having survived so far in my complicated parallel worlds without any major hang-ups. Of course, I was fortunate in having a great marriage and three healthy children. But I too have an Achilles Heel, and it was this that was once almost my undoing.

A few months after Laura was born I found myself pregnant again. This would be our fourth child and I was delighted. By now in my late thirties I was frankly getting old in reproductive terms, but our kids had no extended family so an extra sibling

~ 205 ~

would be a very welcome addition. When I was nearly half way through this pregnancy James's parents generously volunteered to look after the two oldest girls for one week in their own home to enable James and me to have a break before the new baby arrived. They suggested we take Laura, then a one-year old toddler, with us somewhere reasonably inexpensive, a shortish flight from Birmingham, which was their nearest airport. We booked a no-frills mid-week 'cheapie' to the island of Menorca in the Spanish Balearics. Our travel insurance for this break was the most basic one on offer.

Menorca was sunny and we enjoyed watching Laura paddling in the small baby pool. It was a rare opportunity for us to have her all to ourselves. On the second day of this idyll I noticed a single drop of bright red blood on my underclothes. I wasn't particularly alarmed, but felt I ought have a check-up just in case. There was a small basic hospital on the island. None of the staff spoke English, and we certainly spoke no Spanish. A hospital porter who had mastered 'tourist English' was found to act as our interpreter, and I was sent for an ultrasound scan. James was not allowed to accompany me as he had Laura with him and children weren't admitted in the clinic rooms.

When the radiographer passed the probe over my stomach I craned my neck to see the screen, and was reassured by the sight of a small grainy blob which vaguely resembled a baby. A white-coated doctor then entered the room, and after a rapid-fire conversation in Spanish which ensued between the radiographer the doctor and the porter, James, with Laura now mercifully asleep on his shoulder, was summoned into the scan room. The Spanish doctor then asked the porter to translate the following: 'I'm very sorry, there is no heartbeat—the baby is dead.'

We were stunned—completely numb. And he added: 'Also, this pregnancy is not as far advanced as you say—according to the measurements fetal demise occurred at least three weeks ago.' In other words I had been carrying a dead baby inside me for the past month. I was speechless with shock. The doctor, somewhat tediously via the porter/interpreter, informed us that the only re-course was surgery to remove the dead fetus, and that this had to be done soon. He could not vouch for my safety if I discharged myself in order to fly back to Britain for this procedure—the threat of a major haemorrhage mid-air was too great. In any case our basic travel insurance would not cover the cost of medical repatriation. We had no choice but to agree. By now it was nearly midnight, and the doctor was keen to finalise things. James was sent away in a taxi with Laura, and I was sent up to the ward and scheduled for surgery in the morning.

All night long I lay rigid in that hospital bed with my eyes wide open my hands hovering protectively over my slightly rounded belly, willing the inert mound to move, even slightly, to prove the doctor was mistaken. Above my head hung a clipboard with my details. I could just make out the diagnosis which was printed underneath. It read: *Gravid: negativo. Muerte fetal.* My baby was *muerte*. Dead! How could this have happened without my knowledge? What had I been doing a month ago? I shouldn't have lifted that heavy bag…or was it those unripe plums I had eaten…had I overdone hoovering the stairs..? I was racked by guilt and nameless recriminations, unable even to think about praying. God wasn't in this picture at all.

In the morning the patient in the bed next to me smiled sympathetically, and the Spanish nurse who came to prepare me for surgery tried to reassure me via sign language. But I was beyond comforting; I just lay there silent and stiff, like a corpse. Soon I was wheeled away and into the operating room. During this time James was in a hotel some miles away with our one-year old toddler, frantically trying to phone his parents, and to inform the Thomas Cook holiday representative to arrange our flights home.

When I came round from the anaesthetic he was there beside me. Instinctively I put out my hand to feel my tummy—it was now as flat as a pancake. James looked anguished, and I tried to be brave.

The worst of the next few days was hearing babies wailing in the maternity ward next door. At the end of that week we boarded the plane that took us back to Birmingham—we left part of ourselves behind on that sunny Spanish island.

It took me a long time to get over it. It is difficult for me, even now, to describe the obsessive nature of maternal instinct without sounding faintly unhinged. Grief after a death is recognised and respected, but grief for the loss of an unborn baby is quite different. Society conspires to render miscarriage invisible, and it's a terribly lonely place. In addition to all those feelings I also felt terribly guilty—guilty at being unable to put a brave face on it, guilty for not appreciating what I already had, guilty in turning away from God even though I knew that God was a loving Father. I didn't 'deserve' the baby, and it had been taken away. Like many men in a similar situation James was intent on comforting me, but he was confused by the sheer depth of my sorrow, and ultimately frustrated at being a bystander unable to penetrate the web of my despair. And all the while I was still going through the motions of looking after our household while he continued to go to work. I became a zombie wife and mother and was nearing a crisis point.

Exactly what prompted me to take the first step in turning this situation around eludes me. But time is a healer of sorts, and eventually I reasoned that my overriding regret was that this scrap of humanity, which had held all my love but had ended up in a hospital incinerator had never been properly acknowledged. Having children already didn't seem to make it any easier, for I knew exactly what it was that I had lost. Despite James reminding me gently many times over, 'It wasn't actually "a baby",' I felt the need to have its existence formally acknowledged. When I tentatively suggested a brief private service in church, James wasn't keen— it's not his style at all. But I'm grateful that he didn't refuse to go along with it.

I contacted the curate of our episcopal church who didn't bat an eyelid and said he would be more than happy to oblige. So one evening James and I, along with Alice and Mary, aged five and four, met him in the small side chapel of Christ Church in Morningside which had been lit by candles. Robed in a white alb, the minister donned his confessional stole, knelt with us, and said a few simple prayers acknowledging the existence of this child of our union who had not lived and whose soul we now entrusted to God's infinite care. He blessed our family and our marriage and prayed that we would take comfort from the knowledge that everything was part of God's plan. The service was over in a matter of a few minutes, but it had meant the world to me. Our girls were each given one of the candles in memory of their lost sibling. The four of us then went to a nearby café for a bite to eat. The fog of sadness in my head began to lift, and I was able to move on after that, and fairly quickly recovered my usual old self.

And the God of Surprises hadn't finished with me yet. Just a year later, now aged forty, I was back in hospital, sweating and moaning my way through an almost interminable labour. We were finally rewarded by hearing a newborn cry and the words, 'Congratulations, you have a fine son.' A son? It was surely a mistake—we only did girls! But it was true, and when a perfect baby boy was placed in my arms, I wept tears of gratitude and relief. We named our son Andrew after the patron saint of Scotland, and with our daughters he has been the source of much joy in our lives.

⁓⁓⁂⁓⁓

James and I had married in 1980 which was also the year of the American Hostage Crisis. Thereafter diplomatic ties between Iran and Great Britain ceased. My baptism two years earlier in Tehran was not known to the Iranian authorities due to the fear of reprisals from Islamic authorities. But when Baba died in 1992, Mami said that it had been his dearest wish that his half-British grandchildren should be recognised as legitimate in Iran. Iran was now an Islamic Republic and I had been born into a Muslim family and was considered to be a Muslim. However, because I had not married in a Muslim ceremony, I was not officially James's wife but his concubine, and our four children were therefore illegitimate.

Left to right: Laura Alice, Andrew, Mary

To please Mami who had recently been widowed, I decided I would rectify this anomaly. How difficult could it be? It was surely simply a matter of sorting out the paperwork at the Embassy in London. I travelled down to London from Edinburgh by train on the overnight Sleeper. Not possessing a valid Iranian passport and claiming to be already married with four children immediately aroused suspicion at the Embassy.

'My marriage is registered under British civil law,' I said, not adding that I had actually married in a church. 'Here is the certificate.' The official took a withering look at the paper on his counter. 'You Muslim?' he asked, as I remained silent. 'Then you provide Muslim certificate!'

At first this didn't appear too daunting a task. However, getting a Shia' marriage performed in Edinburgh proved to be quite tricky. Iran's official religion is Shia' Islam, whereas in most of the rest of the Islamic world Sunni Islam predominates. Edinburgh's mullahs were indeed Sunni, but I managed to unearth a Shia' mullah in Glasgow, and I duly telephoned him, feeling guilty that I wasn't a Muslim any more but still pretending to be in order to acquire a necessary piece of paper. It felt horribly like double-crossing God. Reassuringly, this mullah agreed to come from Glasgow to Edinburgh to perform the marriage ceremony. 'Would you like me to arrive in Islamic dress, or in Western clothes?' he asked. I was taken aback by this. Was this a test of my allegiance to Islam? I had a brief mental image of a turbaned mullah in flowing robes striding through the streets of genteel Morningside. 'Western dress is fine,' I squeaked.

On the appointed day a battered old car came to a halt outside our house, and out stepped the Mullah, a dapper youngish gentleman wearing a light suit with the obligatory anti-decadent-Western style open-necked shirt. After some small talk and Persian tea, we got down to business. Turning to James he asked, 'Are you a Muslim?' Taken completely by surprise on hearing this unexpected opening gambit, James truthfully replied that he wasn't. 'Oh but this lady you are marrying is, and Muslim women may only marry Muslim men—if you are not Muslim she cannot marry you—that is Shari'a law.' This was a huge stumbling block, and its implications took a while to register. However, the Mullah told us that the situation could be salvaged if James converted to Islam. It was a massive double irony which was not lost on either of us: *a Christian nominally converting to Islam in order to re-marry his wife who was a Christian convert from Islam!* Caught between the nightmare of complicated Middle Eastern bureaucracy, his widowed mother-in-law, and the potential future legitimacy of his offspring, James generously offered to state his belief in the two key pillars of Islamic faith: 'There is no God but One God,' and 'Muhammad is His Prophet,' after which he was officially pronounced a Muslim and given a Muslim name— Muhamad Hossein. We then proceeded to a speedy and simple marriage contract.

~ 211 ~

Weeks passed and we waited in vain for the official marriage papers to arrive in the post. Eventually I telephoned Glasgow. 'Our marriage certificate hasn't arrived yet,' I said. 'Ah,' replied the Mullah, 'the Ayatollah in London says there is a problem.' ('The Ayatollah in London'? I wasn't aware of any ayatollahs in London!) 'You see, Farifteh *Khânum*, Islam is a chaste religion; purity is a virtue in women and a Muslim woman is above all very chaste. However, in your marriage there are four illegitimate children already.' I could hardly contain myself. Had we not already explained that we had married at a time when no diplomatic ties existed between our two countries? That it had been impossible to register our union at a non-existent Embassy? We were at an impasse, and obviously powerless to put the clock back.

'OK, we will find a solution,' the Mullah countered soothingly. 'But it would help if you contribute something to help the worldwide work of Islam.' This, at least, was a familiar face-saver—honour could be satisfied.

When our marriage certificate finally arrived, James took a day off work and we travelled to London together to register our union officially at the Islamic Embassy of the Republic of Iran. James in his guise as the New Muslim Husband made a very favourable impression on the Embassy officials, and he even charmed the Muslim clerics who presented him with a suitcase full of Muslim literature and religious tracts to help his understanding of the true faith. Thirteen years after our lovely church wedding, I was a new wife again, and my husband appeared to have saved his soul.

This ceremony was orchestrated solely to fulfil the requirements of Iranian marriage law at the time. It continues to have no bearing on our personal spiritual faith—we both remain committed Christians.

Nevertheless, dear James never tires of reminding me that he has more than proved his love for me: 'I've married you not just once—*but twice!*'

Our family, Edinburgh, 2012
(back row: Mary, Andrew, Laura, James; front: Alice, Farifteh)

Chapter 12

FOUR LAST THINGS

I have arrived at my final chapter, though I am not yet at the finish line. There have been times in the past when I might have been glimpsed hurtling headlong towards a sticky end, but luckily I've survived thus far with just a few battle scars. Marriage was ultimately the making of me—James has been a wonderfully steadying influence. Of course, I'd like to think that I've enhanced his life, too, even though he is never slow to point out that I've given him more than a few grey hairs over the years! I smile whenever I recall my meeting with Bishop Hassan to discuss baptism all those years ago in Isfahan, and his caution to me that it might preclude marriage. In the years before his death we would joke about it every time we met. Bishop Hassan became almost a father to me, and he was naturally delighted at how things turned out in the end. 'Lesson Number One,' he would say with a chuckle. 'Always listen to God first—bishops don't know everything!" James and I are fortunate that our children have all become strong individuals with decent moral values. In the parenting stakes they would probably admit that Mum was the Iron Lady and Dad the Softie, but I hope this Memoir will have shown them my other sides too.

Why have I called this final chapter 'Four Last Things'? With an apology to Christian eschatology and the study of *The Four Last Things,* there remain four aspects of me which I have not yet mentioned, and this Memoir would not be complete without them. The first is a deeply personal and abstract 'thing' which defies my attempt at a descriptive title—I call it a 'spiritual longing'. The other 'things' are more immediately recognisable—they are my three 'M's: midwifery, music and merriment.

1. *Spiritual Longing*

Thou hast made us for Thyself, O Lord, and our
heart is restless until it finds its rest in thee.

(St Augustine, *Confessions* 1:1)

My heart secretly yearns for a deep closeness with God who is
my heart's 'Beloved'. This longing for Him is really a reflection of
His longing for me. Love draws me inexorably back to Love, and I
long for 'Home', to be at one with Him.

There! I've said it now!

Such a statement would appear to be at odds with the person
whom most people perceive as *me*. It's an abstract yearning which
doesn't seem to be remotely allied with my otherwise robust enjoyment of many earthly things. I don't talk about it. Once or
twice I've attempted to put it into words, but the harder I tried,
the more I began to sound like a religious fanatic! A truly intimate
connection with God has been rare, but on fleeting occasions I
may have come close, and inexplicably moved to tears at the
glimpse of such exquisite grace. The anonymous mediaeval Christian mystic, author of *The Cloud of Unknowing*, voices it eloquently:

> He may not be known by reason, He may not be got-
> ten by thought, nor concluded by understanding;
> but He may be loved and chosen with the true lovely
> will of thine heart...

> Press upon Him with longing love...
> ...then will He sometimes peradventure send out a
> beam of ghostly light, piercing this cloud of unknow-
> ing that is betwixt thee and Him.

(*The Cloud of Unknowing*, c.1375)

I don't understand this yearning, but for as long as I can remember it has been an inviolable part of me. Baba was a Muslim who secretly leaned towards Sufi mysticism. We never had the opportunity to discuss it before his death, but perhaps I have inherited something akin to it from him.

2. Midwifery

Like everything else in life I came to midwifery late, but it is the profession which best defines me because I worked as a hospital midwife until I retired. When our four children were aged seven, nine, twelve, and thirteen, I decided to return to nursing. I rapidly discovered that the days of readily available part-time NHS posts that favoured working mothers were past. In any case, I had taken fifteen years out of the profession to raise a family and my nursing qualification was now 'time-expired'. The only available vacancy for a Back to Nursing course was in Aberdeen one hundred and fifty miles away. Having no family members to help facilitate childcare I was unable to take up the offer, so I decided to retrain as a midwife instead. The midwifery diploma course at the Lothian College of Health Studies in Edinburgh was then eighteen months for qualified nurses.

In the United Kingdom midwives are state certified practitioners who implement and deliver the entire spectrum of care in normal pregnancy and childbirth. They are fully accountable by law for their own practice and caseloads. Five pregnancies and four babies in rapid succession was perhaps reasonable 'street cred' for a middle-aged entry to the 'Midder', as it was known. History repeated itself when I became an older student midwife. This time, however, the age gap was such that I could have easily have passed as the mother of some of my fellow-students! Additionally my brain had been somewhat addled by years of being a mum at home and I found getting back into study mode wasn't easy. It was especially difficult to be coming home from work bone-tired and just wanting to fall into an armchair with a cup of tea, but instead having to make the dinner and supervise homework! After James and I had done the dishes and the kids were finally in bed, I had to motivate myself to burn midnight oil in front of textbooks on female anatomy and physiology. Healthcare had moved firmly into technological spheres, and much of it was now governed by computers and machines, of which I had zero knowledge. I lost count of the number of times I sought advice from my teenaged kids about computer basics during my 'Midder' training. Making the leap from a manual typewriter and card index systems to complex electronic keyboards, hospital confidentiality-encrypted passwords and the Internet was a hugely scary thing. My fellow-students who had all grown up with computers never quite appreciated the difficulties I faced daily.

Somehow I survived, and I gained my diploma as a Registered Midwife at the age of forty-eight. After qualifying, I got a job as an NHS midwife at the prestigious Simpson Memorial Maternity Pavilion in Edinburgh. I loved my job. After two years of working full-time in gruelling twelve-and-a-half-hour shifts, I was able to land a part-time contract, though being a full-time mum on the side meant that my life was still exceptionally busy.

In the early 1990s it was decreed that all nurses and midwives in the UK must be educated to university degree level. I was informed that this also included me. I already had two degrees, but I was told that if I wished to stay in the profession I must possess a university degree that was at the very least related to some aspect of healthcare, which neither of my degrees was. It was probably pig-headed of me but, with a BA and PhD already under my belt, I refused point-blank to become an undergraduate again! I don't think the Nursing and Midwifery Council really knew what to do about it, but I was eventually allowed to bypass the well-trodden BSc route and skip forward at a relatively junior level to attempt the Master of Science in Midwifery Studies at Napier University. It took another two years of nightly endeavours for me finally to graduate MSc Midwifery at the ripe age of fifty-two. I was now a fully qualified Graduate Midwife Practitioner—and with *three* degrees to boot! I stayed on at the Simpson for another ten years, retiring at sixty-two.

Of my seventeen years in the NHS, fifteen were spent as a midwife, so the profession does define me somewhat. People who don't know my 'other' background assume that I've always been a midwife, and that my husband and I met working in hospitals. They are invariably surprised to discover that the reality is quite otherwise. In the context of the whole of my life midwifery has been but a recent ripple.

3. Music

For the first fifty years my life I was completely non-musical. I loved music, but learning to play an instrument wasn't on my radar at school. Music wasn't a subject that my parents considered to be 'useful' like languages, Typing, or Domestic Science. Just as Latin had passed me by, so Music did too. I admired friends who took lessons in piano and violin, but sadly I wasn't one of them. I do remember Mami telling me that her father, the redoubtable *Aghâyé Doktor*, had in his youth played the *târ* (a traditional Persian stringed instrument), so perhaps there was some potential for music in my genes.

When we were first married, James had a season ticket to Scottish Opera in Glasgow and we attended many notable performances together. Sitting high up in 'the gods' I would peer into the orchestra pit during the interval and James would name the various instruments for me—I was so ignorant back then that I was hardly able to identify any! James had been a good singer and a trumpet player at school. Much later he took up the double bass (contrabass), and he is now proficient on this instrument.

With our children it became clear fairly early on that they all had a great facility with music. During their school years they each learned several instruments, progressing to a high standard and winning a number of medals and prizes along the way. Two of them are now professional musicians—Mary is a cellist, and Andrew a jazz double bassist, and both Alice and Laura are able amateur violinists. Of course, there was a price to pay for this expertise in terms of family dynamics. I make no apology for underlining the fact that the onerous task of ferrying the kids to and from music lessons and constantly supervising endless music practice fell to me. Each child had at least two music lessons every week after school on at least two different instruments—they all learned piano, Alice and Laura also had violin lessons, Mary learned the cello, Andrew the double bass and the Scottish bagpipes, and Laura additionally had singing lessons. Our old upright piano (the same one that James had bought instead of a bed in Glasgow all those years ago) stood in the same room as our television set, and I made it an iron-clad rule that the TV was never to be switched on until all the children had done their homework and completed their piano practice. The more conscientious among them would get annoyed at their dawdling siblings, and loud protestations of 'It's not fair!' would reverberate around our house most evenings before James came home from work!

However, I digress. The result of all this activity was that I thought perhaps I, too, had the ability to learn music—I certainly was keen to try. James's timely advice was that if I was going to learn from scratch in later life I shouldn't choose a 'popular' instrument as the competition for places in amateur orchestras would ultimately be fierce. The available choices boiled down to the bassoon or the viola. I wasn't able to make any sound blowing through a double reed, so I chose the viola.

The viola resembles a big violin, and its pitch range is between that of the violin and the cello. Because of its larger size, and the fact that it plays music written in the unique alto clef, it is by no means an easy instrument to master or to play comfortably. I began lessons with my kids' violin teacher. In fact, I'm still having lessons! But now I've progressed to a standard that enables me to play in orchestras. And I absolutely love it.

There is something magical about the discipline and hierarchy of a symphony orchestra where each instrument has its own leader and there is a desk order within each string section loosely based on ability. Members within each instrumental unit must work as a unified whole. Violas sit right in the centre of the string section, between the violins and the cellos, and play the middle registers. They don't project as distinctively as the upper strings, but leave them out and the music is like a feast without wine. Occasionally they are given achingly beautiful solos; but unlike their showy neighbours who often clamour for the limelight, violas are usually playing in the middle of the orchestra providing the essential harmonies and responsible for the music's rhythm and texture. The particular strength of the viola is fully revealed in chamber music where it has its own solo voice and therefore a much greater overall responsibility. Playing in a string quartet is absolutely my favourite pastime. Letting my viola soar with an occasional melody in its uniquely rich timbre obviously appeals to a latent exhibitionist streak. When string quartet music is played well, the music becomes a sublime thing, almost on a par with the angels of heaven.

As a late starter I usually sit at the very back of the viola section in an orchestra, just forward of the noisy brass. I can no longer read the music without my special music specs whose prescription is set to focus on a 'middle distance' measured from my seat to the music stand, hence my view of the distant conductor is often somewhat blurred. These are physical inconveniences not usually appreciated by the 'wunderkinds' in the front desks. In a string quartet on the other hand, the setting is very intimate with just four players, so the physical logistics are much easier to manage. If you ask my children they will tell you that they have endured years of dreadful viola practice, and that, moreover, it's still on the go! It's all right for them to talk—they have the technical facility of youth and the ability to play almost anything well on their respective instruments with apparently minimal effort. But for me, in terms of sheer enjoyment, learning to play the viola continues to be worth all the frustration, effort, and finger callouses.

4. Merriment

I love to laugh, and I laugh often. Nothing is quite as delicious as laughter in good company. This trait will surprise people who know me only as the 'serious' mother, midwife, or churchgoer. Those who know me well can vouch for my great love of humour, my delight in the ridiculous, and my enjoyment of the comical and absurd. I find laughter infectious; it triggers an instant sense of intimacy and happiness, and is a great means of connection with complete strangers. Shared laughter at all sorts of funny nonsense has kept my relationship with our adult children fresh and exciting. This merry trait belongs more to my Persian roots than to my *farangi* side, as British humour is often 'dry', restrained, tongue-in-cheek. Middle-Eastern attitudes to humour are quite different—people poke fun unrestrainedly, though never completely insensitively, at their own and everyone else's foibles. A sense of humour definitely helped us in the midst of the post-revolutionary *harj-o-marj* in Iran when the future seemed all but hopeless.

In the orchestral world viola players are often the butt of the so-called 'viola joke', a stereotype for numerous gibes among musicians. The more masochistic and good-natured amongst us viola players are actually keen tellers of such jokes ourselves, and it says a lot for our general stoicism that these are borne with dignity and good humour. I love good viola jokes and really enjoy repeating them. It is perhaps something to do with an innate ability to laugh at myself—after all, nobody is perfect, least of all me.

Mami used to say, 'If you don't learn to laugh at your troubles, you won't have anything to laugh about when you grow old.' And that is certainly true, for old age is definitely not for cowards.

Failing memory, stiff joints and bits of one's body that don't function well anymore are perhaps no joke. But since physical decline is inevitable, describing its minor inconveniences can actually be quite comical. I am probably becoming less inhibited about such matters and more confident in wearing my heart openly upon my sleeve. I am also now able to indulge in lots of hilarity and jolly nonsense with my young grandchildren without the fear of censure—they invariably adore a funky granny! Dare I hope that when my end comes I may go out with a bang rather than a whimper? I would love my funeral to include a few laughs—the only real regret being that I wouldn't be around to join in!

Gentle Reader, I have now reached the end of this Memoir, but I am not yet done with life and some adventures surely still lie ahead.

I hope you will think of me as someone who loved life, lived it at full throttle, and yet longed to be 'Home' with God.

When all is said and done, at my very end it might simply be that

> Because I could not stop for Death,
> He kindly stopped for me;
> The carriage held but just Ourselves
> And Immortality...

> (Emily Dickinson, 1890, *posth.*)

THE END

Family visit to Iran, August 2001
(left to right: Andrew, Lilli, Laura, Mami, Alice)

Postscript

In August 2001, just before the events of 9/11 radically altered the West's relations with Islamic countries, James and I and our four children, then aged eleven, thirteen, sixteen and seventeen, travelled to Iran for two weeks. This was my first visit in twenty years. No longer possessing a valid Iranian passport, I chanced my luck and applied for visa with my British passport.

In Britain my nationality status is that of a dual citizen. However, there is a perennial problem in that Iran does not officially recognise 'dual' citizenship as such. In the present climate of strained relations with the West, this fact, to say nothing of my conversion from Islam, nor the headache of my academic grant under the Shah's government, conspires to make us cautious. Mami, now a widow in her nineties and living in Tehran, is ever-fearful of retribution. While such a fear is perhaps unfounded, the questions surrounding this whole situation are not particularly conducive to peace of mind for any of us.

Nevertheless, in the summer of 2001 my British passport was simply processed along with everyone else's and I obtained the required visa. Our visit was truly wonderful. Iran is a historical country, bursting with amazing architecture and cultural sights — an absolute delight for discerning tourists. Persian hospitality is second to none, and we were welcomed everywhere with genuine interest and affection. Mami and Lilli were able to accompany us as we all visited Isfahan, Shiraz and the ruins of Persepolis together. In the twenty years since I had left, Iran had undergone massive changes and Tehran was no longer the wrecked town that I remembered from 1979. Green parks abounded everywhere and the metropolis was buzzing, though the city's traffic was even more horrendous than I recalled. But Iran was now an Islamic republic and a modest dress code was strictly enforced, which our girls found trying in the heat. Wearing the *châdor* was a particular chore, and they were embarrassed to be constantly ogled by onlookers curious to see these blonde *farangis* struggling to keep one end of the unwieldy tentlike garment firmly on their head while preventing its hem from trailing in the dirt.

I was naturally absolutely delighted to meet my family again, but it didn't really feel like 'coming home'—in fact, it felt as though I was an interloper. As ever, I was unable completely to throw off the mantle of never quite fitting in. Fortunately, with a *farangi* husband in tow I could explain that it was in deference to him that I had adopted my *farangi* ways.

Mami and Lilli

We returned home from this visit with many positive feelings, sustained by wonderful memories, and reassured that Iran was finally opening up to tourism. A few weeks later, however, the cataclysmic events of 9/11 changed everything. Iran would soon acquire the soubriquet 'Axis of Evil', and its relations with Europe and America would harden further. I cannot say that they have recovered.

Lilli now lives with her second husband in the town of Rasht, not far from the Russian border. She has led a very different life from mine, a much more difficult one. Not only was she pulled alive from the massive earthquake which struck northern Iran in 1990, but she was also deeply affected by what happened to her during the Revolution; and as result she feels unable to visit us in Britain. We remain worlds apart—affectionate strangers, with just a shared bond deeply forged in our *farangi* childhood. Lilli travels often to Tehran to be with Mami, but as neither of them appears to possess a computer our communications are perforce limited to the telephone. It is really only through the auspices of younger family members that either of them has seen a recent photograph of me—and apparently Mami's reaction to my grey hair was slightly less than complimentary—few Persian women embrace the *farangi* custom of ageing completely naturally!

By now I have lived in Scotland for almost half of my life, yet when people ask me where I'm from I still find it impossible to give a concise answer, and always begin by first taking a deep breath! After years of attempting to be considered mainly *farangi* rather than Persian, I am now of the opinion that I'm actually neither one nor the other but a true hybrid.

Following retirement my life has been remarkably settled. Our four children have grown up and flown the nest. Alice and Mary are married. Alice is a school teacher in Edinburgh with children of her own. Mary lives in New York, and Andrew is based in London—both are professional musicians. Laura, engaged to be married in 2017, presently works in Human Resources in Newcastle-Upon-Tyne. James and I continue to live happily in Edinburgh where we have worked and raised our family. We are enormously proud of our children and everything they have achieved, and we're truly fortunate to be able to see them all regularly and to have remained part of their lives.

Despite many shortcomings I've never wavered from my adopted faith, and it will soon be forty years since my baptism in Tehran. Christ Church, the lovely Scottish Episcopal church in Morningside, Edinburgh, has become my spiritual home. I sometimes worry that the ardent and enquiring spirit of my youth, which yearned so single-mindedly and against so many odds for Christ, may be transmuting into a Mrs Comfortable Morningside—I must ensure that it never does.

More than a hundred years spans the birth of my parents and that of my grandchildren—a century during which my own life unfolded. This Memoir will have shown them a glimpse of that life and their past heritage.

Appendix A

TIMELINE

TIMELINE

	1905	Baba's birth, Semnan
World War I	1914–1918	
	1922	Mami's birth, Tehran
'Modernisation' of Iran by Reza Shah	1925–1935	
Chador banned in Iran	1936	Baba travels to England
World War II	1939–1945	
	1947	Mami travels to England
	1948	Baba and Mami's marriage, Birmingham
	1949	Baba and Mami settle in Geneva
	1950	Farifteh's birth, Geneva
	1952	Lili's birth, Geneva
	1965	Baba retires from WHO; Hafezi family relocates to Tehran
	1968	Farifteh graduates from French Lycée, Tehran
	1972	Farifteh graduates BA English, National University of Iran
	1976	Farifteh and James meet, Nottingham
	1977	Farifteh graduates PhD English, University of Nottingham. Returns to Iran; Appointed Lecturer, National University of Iran

Riots and mass demonstrations in Iran; Imposition of martial law	1978	Farifteh's baptism, St. Paul's Church, Tehran
Islamic Revolution in Iran; Monarchy overthrown; American Hostage Crisis	1979	Farifteh begins Student Nursing, London
Iraq invades Iran	1980	Bahram Dehqani-Tafti murdered, Tehran; Farifteh and James's marriage in Nottingham; Move to Glasgow
American hostages released	1981	
	1982	Farifteh and James move to Leeds; Farifteh appointed Nurse at St James's University Hospital
	1983	Birth of Alice, Leeds
	1984	Birth of Mary, Leeds
	1985	Farifteh and James's year in Grenoble, France
	1987	James appointed Consultant Orthopaedic Surgeon in Edinburgh; Farifteh and James move to Edinburgh
		Birth of Laura, Edinburgh
	1990	Birth of Andrew, Edinburgh
	1992	Baba's death, Tehran
	1993	Farifteh and James's Muslim marriage certified, Edinburgh
USA imposes trade ban with Iran	1995	
	1996	Farifteh commences midwifery training, Edinburgh
	1997	Farifteh appointed Midwife at Simpson Memorial Maternity Pavilion, Edinburgh
9/11 tragedy in USA	2001	Robb family visits Iran
	2002	Farifteh graduates MSc Midwifery, Napier University, Edinburgh
	2012	Farifteh retires from the NHS

A BRIEF OUTLINE OF CHRISTIANITY IN IRAN

On the Day of Pentecost it is known that Parthians, Medes and Elamites were among the crowd listening to Peter preach in Jerusalem (*Acts* 2:9). St Simon the Zealot and St Thomas are thought to have been the first apostles to bring the gospel to Persia. For several centuries Christians in Iran consisted only of believers belonging to ancient Eastern Orthodox rites. Armenians and Assyrians were its main adherents, and each group retained its distinct ethnicity, culture, and language within the Persian population. After the coming of Islam in the seventh century these churches survived unscathed, protected by the new Muslim rulers. Armenian churches particularly flourished in Iran following the Ottoman persecutions of the early twentieth century. Armenians and Assyrians are Iranian Christians, but with their own ethnicity and cultures they have remained separate from the indigenous 'Persian Church' which emerged in the wake of Protestant evangelism in the nineteenth century.

In 1812 Henry Martyn, an English missionary in India, translated the New Testament and Psalms into Persian—the language which at that time was a *lingua franca* from Damascus to Calcutta. In order to have his work officially recognised, Martyn was obliged to present it to the ruler of the day, Fath'Ali Shah, with the help of the British Ambassador. Missionaries who later came to Iran would also require the representative support of their respective governments to establish Christian hospitals and schools among the Persians. The new Persian Church was therefore early on perceived to be affiliated with foreign powers—an alliance that would ultimately become an obstacle to its expansion.

British and American missionaries established a number of Christian institutions in Iran in the late nineteenth and early twentieth centuries through which the Christian message was propagated. A significant Anglican presence arose from the efforts of missionaries sent by the Church Missionary Society. The *farangi* Christian hospitals and schools were respected, appreciated, and increasingly used by local people. Through patient evangelism a truly Iranian Church began to emerge. Unlike its Armenian and Assyrian counterparts this Iranian Church was primarily Persian and Protestant, with a core of converts from Muslim, Jewish and Zoroastrian backgrounds.

By the middle of the twentieth century the Episcopal Church In Iran was reasonably well established. Today it is one of four large member dioceses within the Anglican Province of Jerusalem and the Middle East—the others are: the Diocese of Egypt and North Africa (including Algeria, Tunisia, Libya and the Horn of Africa), the Diocese of Cyprus and the Gulf (including the Arab States in the Gulf, Arabia and Iraq), and the Diocese of Jerusalem (including Lebanon, Syria, Jordan, Palestinian Territories and Israel). The first Persian Bishop was Hassan Dehqani-Tafti, a convert from Islam, who was consecrated in Jerusalem in 1961. Bishop Hassan served in Iran for twenty-five years. He was followed by Bishop Iraj Mottahedeh, and subsequently by Bishop Azad Marshall. In common with other churches in the Anglican Communion, the basis of this church's liturgy is the *Book of Common Prayer* translated into the vernacular, Persian (*Farsi*).

The Islamic Revolution of 1979 dealt a severe blow to this small but thriving church. In February 1979 its senior priest, Reverend Arastoo Sayyah, was murdered in Shiraz. Christian schools and hospitals were taken over by local revolutionary committees. Missionaries left the country, or were briefly imprisoned. Bishop Hassan's protests to the new Islamic authorities fell on deaf ears. In Isfahan there was an attempt to murder both him and his wife Margaret, which was thankfully unsuccessful, though in May 1980 their only son, Bahram, was shot and killed by revolutionaries in Tehran. An attempt was also made on the life of the Diocesan secretary, Jean Waddell.

Today the Diocese of Iran differs from others of the Middle

Eastern Province in that its small congregations no longer have any affiliated institutions—all have been expropriated by the Islamic regime. The 'Faithful Remnant' in Iran consists of four main congregations in Tehran, Isfahan, Julfa, and Shiraz who continue to gather faithfully for worship and fellowship, albeit with a fairly muted presence. The organisation, *Friends of the Diocese of Iran* (FDI) unites a diaspora of Iranian Christians abroad, keeping them in touch with Christians in Iran through regular meetings, fellowship and prayer. Its occasional newsletter, *The Mustard Seed*, is circulated worldwide.

A new generation of Christians is now emerging both in Iran and among the Iranians abroad, many of whom are not Episcopalians. Evangelical organisations such as the ELAM Ministries (named for the Persian Elamites of ancient Sumeria, and not to be confused with the similar sounding 'Elim' Pentecostal Church), as well as the popular satellite Christian broadcasting channel, SAT-7 PARS, a vital platform for *Farsi* speakers everywhere, are ushering in a new era of Iranian converts from Islam. This proselytising has led to a proliferation of 'underground' house churches in Iran, and fundamentalist Iranian pastors eager to spread their faith. One reason for such a growing attraction may be that the Persian identity is not completely rooted in Islam, and there is now some disenchantment with its repressive regime, especially among the country's youth. In Britain, too, there have been many recent baptisms of Iranians within the Anglican Church.

Meanwhile, the 'Faithful Remnant' and members of the Iranian Episcopal Church in exile continue to meet quietly and to worship regularly, as they have always done, in the hopeful expectation that from the mustard seed a mighty tree may yet some day flourish.

.

Appendix C

MAP OF IRAN

Appendix D

ADDITIONAL PHOTOGRAPHS

Baba and Mami

Khanum Bozorg (Mami's mother)   *Aunt Mehri (Baba's sister)*

Engaged (January 1980)   Bahram Dehqani-Tafti (1955-1980)

Married (May 1980)

Nursing in Glasgow (1982)   *A year in Grenoble, France (1986)*

Bishop Hassan with James and Andrew (1999)   *Lilli and Mami*

Appendix E

GLOSSARY

PERSIAN	**ENGLISH**
âberu	dignity
âgha	gentleman, sir
Aghâyé Doktor	'Mister Doctor'
Aghâyé Senâtor	'Mister Senator'
amu	uncle
amu-jân	'Uncle Dear'
andarun	inside, interior
avval	first
biruni	outside, exterior
bâbâ	daddy
bacheh	child
bacheyé avval malé kalaghé	'the first child belongs to the crows'
bâdemjân	aubergine, eggplant
bâghlavâ	baklava, a sweet pastry
bâlâ	above, high
balâl	corn on the cob
bârân	rain
bazaar	market
bé-dar	to the door, 'be gone!'
bozorg	great, important
châdor	traditional full-length veil covering the body
Chaharshanbeh-suri	'Red Wednesday', ancient Persian festival of fire on eve of last Wednesday of the year
dâr-al-f'noon	institution of higher learning (an Arabic term)
doogh	a fizzy yoghurt drink

dowreh	circle, a social gathering
droshkeh	open horse-drawn carriage
eid	festival
Farang	(from *'Frank'*) a generic term for 'Europe'
farangi	European, a Westerner
farsang	Persian measure of distance equivalent to about four miles
ghâshogh-zani	'spoon-beating', touring the streets, banging on pots and asking for treats— as part of the Chaharshanbeh-suri festivities
ghismat	destiny, fate, 'kismet'
hâfez	protector
Hâfez-e-Seheh	(*Arabic*) 'Protector of Health'
haft-seen	'Seven S s', the arrangement of seven symbolic items beginning with the Persian letter *seen* (S) traditionally displayed at Nowruz
harj-o-marj	disorder, anarchy
hamshireh	person suckled at the same breast
hichi	nothing
kalâgh	crow
kalântar	policeman
kalântari	police station
khânum	lady, madam
Khanum-Bozorg	'great lady'—a respectful term
khâneh-takâni	'house shaking', spring-cleaning
khoresht	stew
korsi	low table overthrown with blankets with a heater underneath it (traditional home heating)
maktab	traditional school, usually an elementary school
mâlé	belonging to
matrood	outcast

mirza	nobleman, an honorific title
monkerât	morality or 'purity' police
Montakhab-al-Atteba	'chosen among physicians' (an Arabic term)
nân	bread
Nowruz	Persian New Year
najess	unclean
pâ-een	below, inferior
Pahlavi	the last royal dynasty in Iran, also: a gold coin
pasheh	mosquito
pasheh-band	mosquito net
qanât	ancient underground water-supply system
raft	has gone, went
rammâl	geomancer, fortune-teller
rastâkheez	resurgence, resurrection
sabzi	sprouting greens
samanu	a sweet paste
samovar	tea urn
sarafan	pinafore
SAVAK	Persian acronym for 'Organisation of Intelligence and National Security'
seeb	apple
seer	garlic
senjed	dried oleaster fruit
seezdah	thirteen
Seezdah-bé-dar	'Thirteen be gone!', the final day of the Persian New Year festivities, traditionally spent outdoors with a picnic
serkeh	vinegar
seyyed	descendant of the prophet Mohamad, an honorific title
shah	king
shomâl	north
sofreh	tabletop arrangement

somagh	sumac
tameshk	sour blackberry
tanoor	bread oven
târ	string, (cf. 'guitar', 'sitar'), also a traditional Persian stringed instrument
tariâki	drug addict
torshideh	'soured', on the shelf, old maid
urdu	military camp
yakh	ice
yakhchâl	'ice pit', refrigerator
yakhi	seller of ice
zir-zameen	'underground', basement room